The *Five Secrets*
Of a Sales C.O.A.C.H.

BY HILMON SOREY AND CORY BRAY

TABLE OF CONTENTS

INTRODUCTION

Coaching is the activity that has the greatest impact on individual human performance in a team setting, and that's especially true in sales. A sales coach observes performance, identifies a challenge, and works to rapidly make an individual better.

We've seen performance completely transformed by just a few coaching conversations at every level of experience. Veteran sellers who may have been reluctant to adapt to change, account executives who were developing and honing closing skills, and sales development reps challenged by balancing quality and quantity of activity are just a few examples.

This book follows Arlo, the main character, as he sets out on a quest to become a great sales manager. Poorly equipped for success by his current organization, a chance encounter leads him down the path of enlightenment as he learns how to C.O.A.C.H.

The first few chapters of this book set the stage, outlining an all-too-familiar pattern of Arlo, a junior sales manager who wants to do big things, but who doesn't have the training, leadership, and mentorship within his organization to get where he wants on his timeline. In chapter 6, he learns a critical framework to measure rapport with his team. Then, in chapters 7-12 we observe as Arlo learns each element of the C.O.A.C.H. framework. At the end of the book, we summarize Arlo's findings and then point to additional resources, including a coaching workbook and a special offer from ClozeLoop University.

The characters and scenarios in this book are an amalgamation of many we have worked with across various industries, sales motions, and company sizes, and you'll definitely recognize some of their traits. We intend for this book to be digested easily, shared readily, and applied quickly by those who need it.

Now, let's get ready to C.O.A.C.H.

1

THE PATH

"Shame!" shouted a shrouded face in the shadows, joining the chorus of cackling onlookers.

"Shame!" they yelled in his face, one by one, as Arlo walked by them. Their faces were a blur. There were sixty or a hundred of them, he wasn't sure. On either side of him, they pointed and jeered. Every now and then, one would jump in the path just ahead of him and snap a picture with their phone and dash back into the shadows before he could see their face.

SHAME!

The light at the end of this valley of accusers grew closer, and he cowered, afraid that the taunts would grow louder if he ran. He could almost make out his defeated reflection in the polished cement floor beneath his feet.

One foot before the other. He knew that he deserved this. He had let the whole company down.

Arlo's arms held a cardboard box with his belongings—nothing substantial really. Some headphones, a few books, a "Welcome, Rock Star!" plaque he had received on his first day . . . just a few months ago.

There was some company swag he had considered leaving behind, but he didn't want to seem ungrateful. He would have left it all if he had known that he was going to be subjected to this sort of humiliation.

"Shame!" There were more voices behind him than ahead now. The light ahead was growing brighter. It reminded him of the taunting sound of slot machines and the blazing sun ahead when you're finally leaving a Vegas hotel.

He was being perp-walked. He'd blown it. The numbers told the story of utter failure.

"Get out!" The final voice, deeper than the others. It came from a tall, unmasked person he recognized. "You'll never work in this . . ."

Buzz—Buzz—Buzz.

Buzz—Buzz—Buzz.

The alarm jarred him awake and Arlo sat upright with a panic-filled gasp. His ears still rang with the chants of "Shame!"

It was 5:30 a.m. Typically an early riser, the recurring nightmare tempted Arlo to hit snooze. He had no intention of going back there. Not ever.

He'd gotten home late the night before, as the sales team went through the motions in hopes of a miraculous and heroic end-of-month finish. But that never came to pass.

He sighed as his feet hit the cold wood floor. From his bedroom window, he noticed that the city was still asleep, with street lamps lighting an empty stage at every corner.

The little apartment on Tower Hill was his source of pride. He had vowed that by thirty he would no longer live with roommates, sharing food and bathrooms, and time—precious time. There was too little time for him to waste it on beer pong, darts, and online dating chats with people whose pictures and profiles seldom matched the person who showed up on the date.

He had a serious job with serious goals, and he was serious about meeting them. So, six months ago, when he was promoted to sales manager, he had moved into this remodeled one-bedroom apartment at the top of Tower Hill. The apartment was airy, with several windows that provided ample light. He was a full year ahead of schedule. Quite literally moving on up.

His father's military-like discipline and early-to-rise mantra had eventually rubbed off on Arlo. The quiet of mornings were now his favorite time of day. Weaving through the short hallway to the bathroom, the near-empty apartment echoed as he padded across the floor. His mom had snuck him a couch from storage when he moved in. It was not the greatest couch. It looked more like something that had been left behind by a previous tenant than something someone would have willingly moved in. But she had meant well; he didn't have anything else, and it was better than sitting on the floor to eat.

Even though he finally had a place all his own, he still liked the AirPods for his twenty-minute workout. They usually tuned out all the noise in his head and he could concentrate on the tasks to be done, ideas to implement, strategies to develop, the evaluation of his ability and its impact. Arlo had plans. He had to. He had no choice. He didn't have the dot-to-dot convenience of a lot of his peers. They seemed to just fall into good opportunities in spite of themselves. But, in his case, he had to work hard.

He had memorized a quote that hung above his father's tool bench in the garage:

> *If you don't design your own life plan, chances are you'll fall into some-one else's plan. And guess what they have planned for you? Not much.*

The problem was, his plan wasn't working, and today would be filled with the meetings he most dreaded. It was the first day of the month and, oatmeal in hand, he scrolled through the day's calendar in the blue glow of his laptop. Today was yet another day where Arlo would climb into the gerbil wheel and start running.

It seemed productive until he took the time to look around and realize that he really wasn't going anywhere.

In the management team meeting, he would need to come up with some detailed narrative to spin the fact that his team of salespeople had missed their goal for the second month in a row. Truth was, he was trying everything and had no idea what would work.

However, that answer would not suffice. He hadn't got the job by shrugging his shoulders, and he wasn't one to shirk responsibility or shy away from learning.

It just seemed that since being promoted to management, he had been in a state of constant motion, trying to keep spinning plates from falling. He didn't have a rationale for how his team was going to pull through the quarter.

In his sales team meeting, he would have to figure out how to balance between telling the team that their butts were on the line, and providing supportive motivation and guidance to just . . . get. . . . the . . . job . . . done. He wasn't even certain that it was their fault. There was definitely more he could do as a manager. The team was made up of very motivated, if a bit misdirected, junior salespeople in their first closing role. He felt an overwhelming sense of responsibility to make them successful, or at least give them the best chance to succeed.

Then his individual meetings with the sales reps would begin. The 'check-ins.' He wasn't really sure of the usefulness of these meetings, but Gabe, Arlo's VP of sales, had insisted that weekly one-on-ones were essential for 'knowing your people' and 'managing the metrics.' So he would pretend to be engaged while listening to fanciful stories about prospect conversations, excuses regarding data or leads, and baseless predictions that would have no bearing on actual results.

Is this what management consists of? He had been so ambitious five years ago, when he began his career in sales—as a sales development representative. Fresh off of a year of blogging and traveling all fifty states by car, he had realized two things: (1) He was never going to be a travel writer, and (2) his parents weren't going to give him any money. When a fellow journalism grad from school back in Chicago told him that he had got a job "basically interviewing people all day long," which paid two to three times entry-level journalism roles, he hopped online and started applying for sales development roles.

When he landed that first job at DingDong, the restaurant rating and delivery application, he accepted that he wasn't going to be Hunter S. Thompson, after all. His father was happy that he was working. But, heck, he was not going to keep his job if he didn't have a plan to get prospects to talk to him! And getting them to do that wasn't easy.

If he was able to connect with a live person, many would just hang up. The rest refused to respond to his countless calls and e-mails. But he had found a way. He'd discovered a system that worked for him. His manager at DingDong, Misha, wasn't much older than he was at the time and didn't have a ton of expertise to impart, though his stories of being raised in a post-communist Eastern European village were fascinating. What Misha lacked in experience, he made up for in latitude, because everyone was allowed to just do their own thing. In fact, it was expected. Most folks in Arlo's role didn't last longer than nine months.

Thanks to exhaustive research online, and a bit of trial and error, Arlo fell into a productive routine that included some segmented e-mails, combined with select social media touches and well-placed phone calls. It was gold! Ultimately he found himself getting 15–20 percent of his leads to engage, which was enough to pass qualified conversations to his account executive. He became a sales lead within six months, and the recruiters came calling.

■ ■ ■

It was his consistent willingness to put in the effort that had impressed Gabe when he hired him for the account executive role at VizuData. How Arlo longed for that kind of consistency from someone, anyone, on his team today.

He'd asked for budget from management to buy tools ranging from call recording software to playbooks, dialing software, and outbound e-mailing tools—all toward the goal of automating activity and reporting, so that each member of the sales team could take responsibility for their own results.

Instead, he got a barrage of "technology challenges" or worse. His reps were now automating and increasing the distribution of really bad messages! Marketing said the sales team was "amplifying the suck." He couldn't argue.

Back when Arlo first became an account executive, he'd found himself clinging to the activity he was familiar with from his previous role at DingDong—research, calls, e-mails—repeat. DingDong had a really short sales cycle, with typically one decision-maker in a small business. VizuData, however, had a more complex sales process, even when selling to small companies. Business intelligence was being used effectively in the mid-market and enterprise sectors but it was SMB growth that management was looking for. That's how the company's valuation would soar, and then the investors would keep piling in.

But Arlo didn't know how to have closing conversations with executives in those markets. So his plan was to ensure that he had tons of deals in his pipeline. He kept his focus on the top of funnel activity—calls, e-mails…social touches that he was familiar with and it served him well.

While other account executives on the team sat around waiting for, or scrutinizing, their leads from sales development, Arlo was setting the pace by keeping his funnel full. Weekends were spent sourcing leads while he lounged around in sweats on the couch with ESPN on the television and one of four pepperoni deep-dish pies he had shipped from Pizzeria Uno in Chicago every month. He even invested some of his own money to get a virtual assistant to help with web research.

Since Arlo focused on sourcing his own leads, that left him accountable for the quality of his conversations, and so he came to understand how to be patient, identify pain, establish trust, and navigate stakeholders. Because he had no one to blame. It was a slower process, but ultimately, his pipeline was always fluid— either disqualifying or moving deals through stages—and that impressed management.

Sure, he had a lot of learning to do, but his organization provided ongoing product training and even some sales methodology training, which he took to like a fish to water. He fearlessly applied the sales methodology and came to understand that if he demonstrated rigor with respect to the pain questions, customer stories, sales stages, and exit criteria, management would be happy.

Meanwhile, others on the team seemed to go through the motions—doing feature-and-benefit demos and presentations and sending over discounted proposals in the hope that deals would close by themselves. So many discounts! The margins always got smaller and smaller for them as the quarter-end approached.

Once again, Arlo's consistency offered a greater opportunity in the form of management. He wasn't the top closer. But Arlo was a good choice. He even looked like the male sales executives he had encountered, which was, of course, part of his plan.

He was fit, without looking like a gym rat, and clean-cut, without looking like he took too much effort to do so. He wore the requisite sales leader Banana Republic button-down shirt, dark denim jeans, and Cole Haan sneakers to underscore that anti-corporate attitude without crossing the line. Outside the office he wore a casual blazer as a light jacket, but usually hung it from his chair back in the office so he didn't look like he was trying too hard. He carried a notebook. He noticed early on that managers seemed to take notes in notebooks. Not on laptops. So he bought himself a leather one.

His performance was consistently good. No peaks, but no valleys either. Steady. He put in a lot of hours and therefore had the respect of the team, did what management asked and expected, and volunteered often for projects. If there was one to give, Arlo deserved the management opportunity. He got his chance six months ago.

VizuData had just closed a $35 million series C funding round and was moving into a hyper-growth stage. The expectation was to produce 100 percent year-over-year revenue growth and to triple the size of the sales team over the next twenty-four months. That meant hiring five new people per quarter and getting them on-boarded and ramped to goal attainment within ninety days. The only way to scale effectively was with frontline managers who could manage and grow a team. The small- and medium-sized business segment (SMB) was going to be critical for scale, and Arlo was the perfect management candidate.

Arlo was ecstatic at the opportunity! He never dreamt that his number would be called so fast. He was new and ambitious and, if he was being honest, a little relieved to not have to be on the hook for an individual revenue number every quarter. He felt that the climb to the top of the sales profession had two paths. The individual contributor path toward becoming a high-powered strategic or enterprise account executive, or the management route. He knew that growing people and leading a team really energized him and would get him up and out every morning.

But here he was staring into a bowl of oatmeal as the sun began to light the city and the streetlamps retired for the day. The chants of "Shame!" still rang in his ears. He wished he could just skip the day ahead. *What happened to all of that promise? What happened to the dream?* Was he going to fail?

When Arlo had taken the management position, he had known that he would be the person who created consistently winning teams. Since high school he was always the person chosen as leader of a project group. He knew how to work with people and get the most out of them without begging or pushing. On his basketball team he wasn't the best player, but he worked hard and was consistent. He had the most assists on the team, so it was no surprise that more than any specific sales activity, he wanted to be a catalyst for other people's success.

He knew he could be the manager who recruiters sought out. The one who candidates lined up to work for because it was a privilege. The leader who was talked about in executive circles as being critical to driving company success.

He knew that if he learned from the best, he could continue to climb the rungs of progressively greater responsibility and leadership. So, in his first two months, he had attended a sales management boot camp and a sales enablement conference with speakers that included famous consultants, authors, and sales leaders. He made sure to meet each and every one of them and he asked each of them the same question: "How do you best grow the individuals on a team?"

The answers ranged from the vague "hire slow and fire fast!" to the "inspect what you expect" or "put your people first" It all sounded great! But when he got back to the office with notes and handouts, he found very little of it actionable with respect to people.

He realized that people are not a process. They cannot be acted upon. They must be collaborated with.

Meanwhile, his family was worried that he was spending too much energy on work. Arlo's mom kept asking when he was going to introduce them to his girlfriend. He'd lied. There was no girlfriend. They had broken up months before. He had thought a white lie would put an end to the constant, "It's just not normal for someone your age, alone in the city . . ." conversation. He was wrong.

They broke up because he simply had no time. Success in leadership was a quest. His parents would never understand.

He spent any time that he was not working trying to connect with peers in fast-growing companies like his, which had huge growth expectations and scaling teams. He scheduled mentor interviews with founders and CEOs, sales executives, and venture capitalists, from co-working spaces to skyscrapers . . . anyone who would have him. He sold his video game system and replaced gaming time with reading, and would reach out to the authors he found inspiring for conversations. He would exhaust any and every resource to be successful.

He began to refine what he was looking for, and these conversations started to lend some clarity. It seemed that he could classify the successful people he was meeting into three types of management categories.

There were the "Pilots" who a lot of salespeople respected. These managers were great in the boardroom—citing numbers and trajectories, whipping up slide decks with metrics and projections, lots of charts pulled from the high-powered tech stack they had assembled to automate and collaborate. The sales floor exhibited screens showing everyone's progress toward goals, specific activities, and company revenue. Each sales rep had their own dashboard showing their open opportunities, conversion rates, volume of activity, velocity, and real-time projections. Few conversations were had about anything other than the numbers, and these managers took pride in having a deep understanding of how their organizations were performing and what fuel was necessary to keep the engine running smoothly.

Arlo also met the "Heroes," who a lot of salespeople admired. These managers had been in the trenches before. Quick to share a story of a deal won and thrilled by rolling up the sleeves to help their sales reps close, these managers were sought for their ability to have a quick impact on team performance. They took personal responsibility for the numbers they projected to hit and had no problem hopping on a call or a plane to help one of their reps to bring a deal over the line. Their sales floor was a busy place, with people circulating to and from the Hero's desk for advice and updates; and no time was more exciting than the end of quarter or end of month. The details of the deal won the day in these organizations, and these managers, while seldom taking credit, often took great pride in "showing the team how it's done."

Finally, Arlo met "Cheerleaders," whom a lot of salespeople loved. These managers sometimes referred to themselves as "servant leaders." They led with passion and knew their sales reps' passions too. Not just professional passions, but what made them tick and why they showed up to work every day. These managers pointed out that they were able to motivate folks by their availability and positive attitude. Their sales floor usually had evidence of a theme party, retreat, sales kick-off, or periodic contest.

The Cheerleader was highly attuned to the morale of the team, buffering the lows and raucously celebrating wins. The Cheerleaders prided themselves on the individual connection they had with each member of their team and the ability to get the best out of each of them. They beat the drum for their sales team and frequently championed team concerns.

Ultimately, it seemed that the most successful managers actually embodied a bit of each of these traits. But Arlo felt that even with those who did not lean too firmly to one side or another, there was something significant missing. Surely it would not be enough to manage the data, pull deals over the finish line, or ensure that spirits remained high. What about continuous improvement? A culture of learning and attainment? A means of consistently developing sales reps into progressively more sophisticated roles?

This did nothing to calm Arlo's anxiety. He still had no plan he could easily implement. VizuData seemed willing to invest in his growth, but he didn't know how to take advantage of that opportunity. He feared that if his people did not grow systematically, then neither would he.

So he did what any young manager would do. He combed the nooks and crannies of the internet—from social media to blogs and webinars, scouring posts and comments, reading blogs, and watching online videos.

As streaks of daylight painted the living room floor, time was running out. Arlo quickly cycled through the folders on his drive—where he had gathered tons of tips and tricks along the way, collected in various screen captures and docs, downloaded slide decks, and pdf files. This was an exercise in futility. The few that he actually remembered, he could not find. Those that he found were so far from context that they were literally just taking up space.

He had thirty days to turn it around.

It reminded him of the last time he had played golf with his dad. He had arrived at the course about an hour before his father in the hope that hitting some balls would knock out the rust and help him on the links.

His dad walked up near the end of the bucket and said, "Son, if you didn't bring it with you, you ain't gonna find it here." He was right.

So, Arlo had hit a dead-end. He was in the unenviable position of knowing that there were things he didn't know. He grabbed his backpack and took a deep breath. Eyes closed, he let out a long sigh. Now he understood what was meant by "ignorance is bliss."

2

THE CORTADO

Coach your team to success.

"Excuse me. Is your name Alex?"

Arlo spun around, confused. He had been lost in his thoughts through the entire commute and was having one of those mornings when you just go through the motions on autopilot and suddenly end up where you're supposed to be. Well, he'd gotten as far as the CupAJoe cafe in the GigaTech building at least.

VizuData had recently moved next door. Finally outgrowing the dusty loft in the alley above the Mexican restaurant, they now had a full floor in a building right next door to GigaTech, one of the unicorns in Silicon Valley. GigaTech was the leading platform for Internet of Things (IoT) devices. Any*thing*. If your home security is connected to the internet so that you can turn lights on and off and access points—that's IoT. If you can access your refrigerator from the grocery store—that's IoT. Your fitness tracker, medical sensor, smartwatch, heck—smart anything made up the Internet of Things. GigaTech became the standard on which all things literally ran.

Founded by Noel Kums, the serial entrepreneur, GigaTech seemingly came out of nowhere to outpace decades-old Silicon Valley chip behemoths, mobile platform companies, and even the hardware makers. The interesting thing was that for those who knew, GigaTech was not necessarily the most innovative player in the space. Its marketing was practically non-existent. But its sales team was absolutely world-class. Unlike other Silicon Valley magnets for talent, GigaTech was unique in that it resisted throwing tons of money at proven or pedigreed sales people. Instead, they consistently hired first-rate raw talent and grew them into extraordinary sales professionals. The biggest payday might be down the street, but the best growth experience was at GigaTech.

Arlo loved the proximity to such success. He imagined VizuData following a similar trajectory, and he wanted to be the catalyst, whispered about among the tech elite.

As much as he missed the taquerias and food trucks of the old neighborhood, he was also decidedly happy about CupAJoe Cafe where they actually had a decent pour-over instead of the watered-down swill from the old donut shop.

"I'm sorry?" he said.

"Is your name Alex?" A woman smiled, peering above her over-sized sunglasses while cocking her head as if she already knew the answer. She was probably in her late thirties, and dressed like one of those people who probably seldom wore the same thing twice. At least not in the same year. No yoga pants, or backpack with a company name emblazoned on it. She was considerably shorter than Arlo, even in heels, but seemed to tower over him from below, if that was possible. Her phone was in one hand with one thumb deftly cycling through e-mail. No earbuds corked her ears—she didn't look as though she had the patience to get through an entire song anyway. Her other hand was outstretched, smile waning. "Because if it's not, I think you may have grabbed my cortado."

"Grabbed your what?" Arlo was nervous now and clearly confused.

"Cortado. My coffee. It says 'Alex,'" she said, in a clipped voice, pausing for effect but still managing a smile. Clearly she was in a rush. Arlo looked at the cup in his hand which did in fact say "Alex," then to the counter where his coffee stood with his name for the day, "Rolo," scrawled on the side. They never got his name right at these places.

"I am so sorry," he said sheepishly, handing the cup to her. "I was in my head . . ."

"Busy day already?" the woman said.

"I'm really sorry again," he said, but she shrugged it off. "Yeah. Management team meeting this morning. Going over last month's sales numbers." He tried to save face by lightly dropping some credentials.

"Fun! How did you do?" she said, actually sticking around for a response. Arlo was caught off-guard and couldn't quickly think of a way to blow off the conversation. Or maybe he felt he owed her the truth for having nearly stolen her coffee.

"I've got a superstar on my team who hits her numbers. Then I've got a bunch of folks who are wildly inconsistent. Sometimes they get the job done, sometimes not. But it's completely random. Last month they didn't."

"Random? Well that's unacceptable. You sure you still have a job?" she said. His heart sank because that was not a possibility he had considered. She kept at it, "It sounds like you haven't learned how to coach." This was the last thing he needed. Some random, fancy, coffee drinker pointing fingers at him first thing in the morning.

"I know how to coach," he said with an exasperated and dismissive sigh, remembering all of the talking heads who shared that frontline managers needed to coach their people. He did a quick recall of the things he'd learned in boot camp and online and said, "I have team meetings, individual meetings, training sessions." He was ticking the list off on his fingers. "I review calls and metrics regularly, and everyone keeps me up to date on their numbers. People just don't perform consistently. They aren't growing in their roles." He thought he was defending himself. But he had dug himself a bigger hole.

"That's not coaching. That's just accountability. It sounds like no one has taught you how to coach," she said with a wry smile.

"Rolo?" She looked quizzically at the name on his cup and gently touched his forearm, as if confiding in a friend. "Coach your team to success." She said each word distinctly while searching his eyes for comprehension. He stood there for a minute. The words filled his head. "Coach your team to success". *Who was this Alex woman? What the hell was she talking about?*

He watched her fade out the door past the sea of caffeine-deprived zombies in line. And just like that, she was gone.

3

THE DAY OF DREAD

SMB may stand for small and medium-sized business, but that doesn't mean that our deals need to be small. These prospects spend money when they have a problem to solve.

Arlo didn't have much time to think about the encounter with Alex because, when he reached the elevator, he was joined by Gabe, his boss. An engineering major and former assistant social chairman of his fraternity at A&M, Gabe had hopped off the mechanical engineering career path ten years ago when, as a wide-eyed college grad eager to get into the defense industry, the only job he could find was in internet security sales with a company that liked hiring engineering students. He had convinced himself that internet security was the new defense industry and sales was a process of engineering people. In fact, he liked to whiteboard sales stages as a process flow mirroring "Hooke's Law" applications to shorten or lengthen the sales cycle. No one knew what he was talking about, but the room silently agreed in order to allow Gabe his engineering references rather than endure lectures on physics and elasticity.

Now, Gabe's eyes sat glazed behind his wire-rim frames from the consistent lack of sleep since returning from paternity leave the previous week. He had been in touch throughout his leave—a video conference fixture with an increasingly unkempt beard and what looked to be exactly the same t-shirt at every meeting. His involvement had been more anecdotal than impactful. A demonstration of commitment which rang hollow.

Regardless, Gabe had hired Arlo, so Arlo was overjoyed to have him back. If nothing more than as a much-needed layer between the CEO and himself. Reporting to the CEO as a frontline manager was not the access to power he had thought it would be. Instead, he had ended up feeling woefully inadequate at every chance encounter. The CEO always seemed to ask a question that Arlo was completely unprepared to answer.

"Hey man. It's Hump Day! You ready for this morning?" Gabe said with as much energy as he could muster. Squeezed in the elevator with the morning rush, they stared at the climbing numbers as the floors ticked by.

"Yeah, I've got some clarity on what happened last month with opportunity creation, and some ideas on converting trade show leads." He didn't. But he was so used to these sidebars that he knew pretty well how to keep Gabe at bay. Gabe didn't like to look backward. "Manage through the windshield, not the rearview," he'd say. So there was never much analysis unless the CEO was asking. Even then it would be just a request to build a report.

As much as Arlo appreciated Gabe for hiring him, it was clear from the start that Gabe was not going to be a mentor. Sure, he had worked for a few well-recognized companies, in progressively more important roles, but if you peeled back the covers, you'd notice that he never stayed longer than about eighteen months. In sales terms, that's just about long enough for it to be clear that you're not hitting the numbers. In fact, it's the average tenure of most Silicon Valley VPs of Sales. Arlo suspected that Gabe was a master politician who talked the talk well enough that executive leadership liked him. He could spout sales acronyms like a savant. He never met a slide deck that didn't deserve a little CAC, ACV, LTV, or MRR love. But along the way, he hadn't learned how to develop managers.

It wasn't his fault. It was becoming increasingly clear to Arlo that managers were another breed altogether. It was not enough to have been an effective salesperson. In fact, in many ways, it was easier to only be accountable to your own activity. Moving the herd? Well, that's why border collies are smart and greyhounds are independent.

Gabe's longest tenure was four years in a selling role at the internet security behemoth that everyone talks about. People say he definitely thrived in their well-oiled, proven sales system, which required just execution, not ingenuity. But he'd been riding that pedigree ever since. The remainder of those eighteen-month stints had led Gabe all over Silicon Valley in increasingly higher level roles, but with little other than career progression to show for it.

"We need to figure out how to increase our average deal size. It's critical," Gabe said, tugging on his Patagonia vest and pushing his glasses back on his nose.

"I think we're almost there. We had a lot of learnings this quarter and now we just need to execute," said Arlo, though he didn't necessarily believe it.

"Well, right now with marketing driving inbound, our CAC to LTV ratio is just way too high. There it was! Arlo smiled to himself.

■ ■ ■

8:30 a.m. Management Team Meeting

"I don't want to talk about anything other than increasing our average deal size. What the hell is going on? I just don't get why this is so tough for us to figure out. Half the country has B2B teams focused on small- to medium-sized business sales. It doesn't have to mean small deals. We need average deal size to increase 40 percent in the next three quarters." Arlo's CEO was typically pretty even-keeled. Every now and then, when he felt that the team mistook his even demeanor for complacency, his tone would change. "What's the problem here, Gabe?"

"Well, since most customers are on our lower-tier plans, competitors are forcing discounts, and we are not cross-selling our products effectively. Our CAC to LTV ratio is just way too high. We had a lot of learnings this quarter, and now we need to drive results." This was why Arlo appreciated Gabe. He ran interference when the going got tough. He would tap Arlo for the high-level overview, then package it nicely in management-speak with the credibility that Arlo himself had yet to earn.

"What exactly does that mean, Gabe?" The CEO had locked in. As an MIT data science PhD, that meant he was rolling up his sleeves to dive into the weeds. All the department managers simultaneously looked down at the conference table to avoid crossfire and being pulled into the data theater. It was as if a collective shrug, back slap, and "good luck" rounded the table.

"I'm working with Arlo to ensure that new leads, cross-sell opportunities, and discounting metrics are at a quality and volume that will create enough pipeline coverage," Gabe volleyed. He was good at this, Arlo thought. "It comes down to moving the needle on individual performance."

"Okay, Arlo. So what's the plan?" the CEO said.

"I've got conversations on the calendar with each of the reps, to do a deep dive into their numbers and reverse-engineer where they need to focus on a daily basis to get there by the end of this month," Arlo said. He caught Gabe's quick glance of approval.

"Then what?" asked the CEO.

"Umm . . . then what?" Arlo was stalling for time.

"Yes." The CEO was waiting patiently.

"Then we just . . . make it happen!" Arlo felt like he heard this plan of action before from some expert at a conference. Or was it a comedy routine? Well, it was the wrong answer.

"So, Arlo, it sounds like you'll have some conversations today and make some individual plans. Then check back in this time next month for review? Does anyone else see the flaw in that strategy?" The CEO was searching for eye contact around the table now. That meant Arlo had just recruited the non-combatants with his stupid response.

"I'll work with Arlo this afternoon to make sure we have touch-points, and by next Friday we'll have implemented a strategy which we'll share with you via e-mail." Gabe came to the rescue again.

"Okay. We need to see directionality by the end of this month. Or we'd be foolish to maintain the status quo." Arlo wasn't quite certain what all that meant, but he was sure that he was off the hook for this meeting, and likely have his head in the guillotine for the end of month. That Alex woman had been right!

Gabe pulled Arlo into a small conference room as they left the meeting. He was good at reframing these things and giving Arlo assurance, if not guidance.

"Hey man, you did fine in there. Expectations are really high, and the board is concerned about our ability to move upstream and sell bigger deals," he said.

"Yeah I get it. It's on me. I'll figure this out!" He didn't know how. But he wanted to get away from the conversation and just breathe.

"You got what he was alluding to, right?" Gabe asked gingerly. "If we can't get this on track, we're going to have to make a change. I don't want you to be discouraged or to freak out, but that likely means replacing some of our salespeople with those who have experience selling multiple products and bigger deals, which is new to us. SMB may stand for small and medium-sized business, but that doesn't mean that our deals need to be small. These prospects spend money when they have a problem to solve."

Arlo's eyes shot up from the floor to meet Gabe's. Gabe's mouth was drawn, eyebrows up, and head gently nodding.

"But you're not gonna let that happen!" he said after the gravity of the moment was allowed to set in for a beat.

Gabe squared him off and squeezed his shoulders. "I'm here for whatever you need. Just let me know how I can support you."

So this was why Gabe hadn't made eye contact in the elevator. Replacing salespeople likely meant replacing Arlo too. He suddenly didn't feel very supported.

■ ■ ■

10:00 a.m. Sales Team Meeting

As he sat before his team, Arlo was barely present. In his head, he kept replaying what had just happened. Was he going to be fired? *Fired!?* That was not part of the plan. He didn't lose at Scrabble, much less at life. This was entirely unacceptable.

Feeling a little edgier than normal, he let the silence sit over the conference room as his team fidgeted on their laptops with pensive looks, pretending to send an important e-mail or scrutinize the CRM dashboard. Anything but make eye contact.

For a moment, he resented the fact that his fate was tied to these people. He'd tried everything humanly possible to get this team to perform, and it seemed they were becoming increasingly resistant to his ideas and suggestions.

Arlo knew that regardless of what he said in this meeting, Seth would nod his head in agreement. He would even offer, "Yeah, that makes sense," in solidarity. He had come from a community organizing background and the fact that he had no problem articulating the value proposition for a complex social issue while canvassing for signatures on street corners, in parking lots, and at metro stations had led Arlo to believe that he would have no problem working with prospects he'd never met.

Well, that was wrong. What Arlo had failed to take into account was that Seth would do anything for a cause he believed in. Anything for a change-the-world opportunity. But he had taken this particular job because he had bills to pay. Not because he thought VizuData could make a difference to humanity.

Seth was the meeting champion. He was a great collaborator and always approached work with a positive attitude, wanting to be a team player. But in spite of all of the spoken commitment, he was paralyzed when it came to changing behavior and did absolutely nothing different week after week! Hired four months ago, he had missed his number every single month.

Jackie broke the silence. "Okay, so . . . we definitely didn't get it done last month."

There she went. The Bully. She never missed an opportunity to taunt and antagonize the team. Why wouldn't she? She always made her goal by the third week of the month. No eleventh-hour theatrics. She was always well ahead of the game. Jackie was Arlo's golden goose. He wished he could take some credit for her success, but Jackie had been there before he got the job and, at the rate things were going, would likely be there long after he was gone. She was a standout volleyball player at a top Division I school, and captain of her team. She won . . . all the time. It was in her DNA. At this point she knew how to practice, she put in the work, and had no fear of failure.

He always wondered why she had not been promoted into a management role. Then he had observed the team dynamics. They didn't particularly like her. In fact, they hated her. But she didn't give a damn. It was evident that she had little tolerance for poor performance and she had no tolerance for a mediocre team. She openly questioned activity and call quality out on the sales floor in a way that Arlo wished he could, even though it did little to change behavior.

"How did you only have two discovery meetings today when I had five, and still did some outbound prospecting?" she'd say, her competitive juices flowing. "Oh, you must have been working some big deals." Then she'd taunt, "Oh, but based upon the board, it looks like none of them converted. Strange." And she'd walk away. Arlo would shoot her a disapproving look over his monitor and she'd smirk and go back to work. Bump, set, spike—all by herself.

The team, naive as they were, thought that they were retaliating by refusing to invite her to lunch. They were wrong. She smelled the weakness and fed on that instead, by not only getting to work before them, but working through lunch and then enthusiastically waving goodbye from her desk as they sheepishly filed out the door trying not to be seen. One by one, avoiding eye contact, exactly at 5:30 p.m. "See you tomorrow, guys!" she'd call after them. Arlo even felt a little intimidated by her because she produced far better numbers than he ever had.

If he could channel that killer instinct into something that resembled greater leadership, she would be an amazing asset to the team instead of just its superstar. His fear, however, was that she was either going to run the whole team out of there or she'd have to leave.

Today, Arlo felt the same antipathy for the rest of them that Jackie did. He was in no mood to hear excuses or promises. The blank stares of "wait, what?" bewilderment were not going to cut it. He needed to figure out something fast, and right now, this meeting felt like a waste of time.

"Actually," Jackie looked around the room, "we didn't get it done the month before either."

"Well, you did," Samantha piped in, stating the obvious. "But the rest of us have some work to do." It was a half-hearted mea culpa, but it satisfied Jackie.

Samantha was very talented but clearly had other priorities. It was an open secret that she had taken the sales role to save money to open a hot yoga studio. Most days she would leave by 4:30 p.m., yoga mat in hand, regardless of her numbers. In fact, she was the only person who never took her laptop home.

"I feel like we started strong and then something shifted mid-month," Derek offered. Distracted. That's what Derek was. His head was in the game, but he couldn't focus. He had left college early to take care of his mom and had worked his way up from retail to this job. Arlo had hired Derek. He had given him a chance because he had been so persistent in follow ups during the interview process.

He'd even bragged about him to Gabe and the CEO. Prematurely, unfortunately. He was scrappy as hell, not afraid to try anything. But just a little misdirected. Derek would spend hours planning his discovery meetings based upon a post he saw from someone on social media. This at the sacrifice of meeting with existing prospects or prospecting. Or he'd spend days working out some tip or trick he'd discovered online. Just busy work. Like folding clothes at a retail store. Lots of arranging but no sales.

Lindsay, sitting on video conference, was plain old mediocre. A giant screen of nothingness. She seldom said anything. Maybe because she was the most senior on the team, maybe because she worked on the other coast and felt disconnected, and maybe— Arlo feared the truth in this one—it was because she wasn't really paying attention. She definitely frustrated Arlo more than anyone else.

She was clearly stuck in what he'd heard referred to as the "Frozen Middle." Not bad enough to fire, not good enough to rely upon. It was as though she ran to the finish line and just stood there looking down at her feet every month.

Yeah, she was consistent, but his plan was to be someone who developed people. Built teams. Took the average ones and made them superstars. He wanted her to run through the tape and keep going. It seemed that she had a great deal of personal responsibility. She was accountable and would work to get the job done—but didn't find much personal passion in it.

She had a degree in theater, which her parents had fully supported. The support ended, however, when she finished her masters in London and chose to move to the city instead of returning to her room at home. It would have been impossible to support herself, even with three roommates, on a stage actor's salary, and she had zero interest in teaching at a community college. So she acted her way into this job.

Maximillian still haunted Arlo. He was the first one Arlo had fired. The worst part was that it was Arlo who had hired him. It kept him up at night, wondering what had gone wrong. Maximillian had seemed to pick up on the bad habits of every one of his teammates and, as a result, was never able to produce more than 50 percent of his monthly goal over three months.

Soon the conference room was clouded with the hot air of explanation, finger-pointing, and abdication. Arlo still said nothing, afraid that he'd be unable to suppress the fire that burned inside him. He was the one being measured by the performance of this team. He was the one failing in his duty to lead. It wasn't their fault. Maybe he wasn't cut out for this. Maybe Gabe had made a mistake hiring him. He wasn't yet willing to throw in the towel, but he definitely needed a new plan.

4

THE FORCED ENCOUNTER

Come as a sponge ready soak, not as a rock stuck in place.

The shadows from the ceiling fan pulsed across the room, with the blue light of the moon outside Arlo's window, as he lay with his hands folded over his chest, eyes open. There would be no sleeping tonight. Arlo had learned in college that he could arrive at answers to problems if he just lay still and allowed his mind to work without actively searching for solutions.

So, there he lay. Hours passed with five words dancing through his mind: *Coach your team to success.* He had been thinking about what the woman named Alex had said. Was it some kind of a riddle? Was it just a throwaway line he was placing too much weight on because of the day's events? Or was there real meaning behind it?

He was disappointed in himself for letting the team off with a peppy, "We've got a fresh new month, and a lot of ground to cover . . ." talk. He even thought he'd caught Jackie's eyes rolling, and heard Seth's sigh of relief. But that was all he'd been able to muster at the time.

Arlo lay in the dark searching for the common denominator. All of the strong sports teams he knew of, they did, in fact, have great coaches. Indeed, many of those coaches had won with different players, in different eras, and even in different organizations. What did they do that could apply to his own work?

He knew he was running out of time. The weekend couldn't come soon enough, but tomorrow and Friday were poised to be a painful exercise in trying to manufacture positivity and motivation, knowing that leadership was beginning to whisper that he was not a good fit for management after all.

Meanwhile, this quarter was ticking away. *Coach your team to success.* He had to track down Alex. Maybe she knew something he didn't. So far, this was his best plan.

■ ■ ■

Thursday morning had passed with Arlo lingering around the CupAJoe cafe from the moment it opened with a creepy, permagrin, "Oh you again!" expression fixed on his face, in the hope that the woman named Alex would appear again. To no avail. The staff had begun to eye him suspiciously. Each hour, he would order another drip coffee and casually slink off to the side of the pickup bar. Scared that if he sat down he'd miss her in the crowd, he lingered about, casting furtive glances toward the glass doors each time they opened, like an amateur thief casing the joint. Finally at 9:30 a.m., he skulked out of the doors and up to his office.

He worried that he might never find her again. His time was running out.

■ ■ ■

"Sir, is there something else I can get for you?" The tall, tattooed barista frowned, staring down her nose-ring at Arlo. The staff was significantly more annoyed with Arlo on Friday than they had been the day before. His lingering around was clogging up the delicate balance of the caffeine machine. The ordered chaos of thousands of half-asleep automatons getting their fuel.

"No thanks. I am just waiting for . . ." He stopped as he heard the unmistakable order behind him. *Tall cortado.* He spun on his heels. "Alex!" So much for that Joe Cool savoir faire. He stopped just short of hugging her.

"Hey, Rolo. Looks like you stole someone else's coffee today?" she smirked, with a nod at his cup. It was his lucky day, the first time they had spelled his name right.

"My name is actually Arlo; they usually get it wrong . . ." He sensed her interest waning and didn't want to lose her. "I've been waiting for you. I mean . . . well . . . not waiting. Looking for . . . I mean. Not in a weird way. Just hoping to catch up with you," he managed.

Alex eyed him suspiciously. "Is that right?"

"Well, it's something you said the last time I saw you."

"I told you to coach your team to success," she said nonchalantly, glancing at a new message on her phone. "What happened? You get your ass handed to you on Wednesday?"

It struck Arlo as curious that she specifically remembered that line from their chance meeting. It seemed to add gravity to her words. Maybe she was on to something. People always said things like, "The devil's in the details," but that was not necessarily an informed opinion.

"Actually . . ." He set his coffee down on the pickup bar and wrung his hands. "Yes. I was told that if I can't pull the team across the line this month, they are going to bring in a more experienced team," he said, trying to figure out what exactly he was hoping to gain from this interaction now that it had arrived.

"I told you," she said, folding her arms and waiting for acknowledgement.

"Yes, you did," he offered. "And I need some help."

"How can I help?" she said. She wasn't going to let him off easily.

"Well it seems like you have a theory . . ."

"A theory?! I don't operate on theories. I use proven frameworks. Theories are for academics, not for practitioners," she said.

Arlo wasn't sure he knew the difference, but he knew that he didn't want to screw up this opportunity. "Can you teach it to me? Quickly?"

Her eyes landed on his, searching for something. "So you want the secret?" she said.

It was one of those now or never moments. The last time he'd had one of these, he remembered stealing the ball from an opposing guard in high school and darting out alone on a fast break. He had practiced a one-handed semi-authoritative dunk all year and he knew he had the space to get it done but he'd laid it up against the glass for two. Classy, but he knew that was a moment that would never come again. And he was right.

"Damned right, I do!" he shouted with overblown conviction— like the, "You can't handle the truth!" line from that Jack Nicholson movie. Alex laughed, picked up her cortado, and headed toward the door.

"That's a good answer, Rolo! I'm at GigaTech. Can you come up to forty-five at noon?"

"It's Arlo, and damned right I can!" He maintained the absurd intensity because it seemed to be working. The gaggle of caffeine-seekers in line—with their headphones in place—were completely oblivious anyway.

"Well, alrighty then!" Alex mock-matched his enthusiasm, "I'll be expecting you. Come as a sponge ready soak, not as a rock stuck in place. Sponges expand. Rocks can only chip away. Understood?"

"Yes." Again, he had no idea what she meant, but telling her so did not seem like a good idea. "I'll be there. Thank you." He watched as she bolted through the door and disappeared into the lobby among the rest. He had no idea what was to come, but felt pretty satisfied with his plan thus far. He smiled to himself.

"Sir?" It was the nose ring again.

"Right, sorry . . . I'm leaving," Arlo said.

5

THE FORTY-FIFTH FLOOR

The term 'coach' is used to identify an individual who elevates the performance of another.

Basking in his resourcefulness, Arlo drifted through a completely unproductive morning. His attention kept wandering toward his watch, waiting for noon to come. He batted back a request to participate in an impromptu marketing meeting, fielded a few questions from reps regarding social selling, and spent an hour in a meeting with Seth—listening to his call recordings to try to explain why Seth's habit of thoroughly educating his prospects on discovery calls was killing his conversion rate to demo.

He tried not to be distracted when a handful of employees set up for the monthly birthday celebration, as they did on the first Friday of every month. Jackie had already closed three deals today, more than everyone else on the team combined . . . while the urgency feigned in Wednesday's team meeting seemed to have dissipated for the others.

He did spend a little time on ConnectIn though, trying to piece together Alex's story. It appeared that she had graduated from a Big 10 school with an English degree, and had joined a cloud storage company called Clowdbase fifteen years ago for an inside sales job. He knew Clowdbase. Everyone knew Clowdbase. They were a "tech unicorn." One of those companies that shoots out of the gate as a startup and doesn't look back until they have a multi-billion dollar valuation and successful IPO. They were called unicorns because every venture capitalist wants one, and they're really hard to find! Her profile showed her moving from sales development to account executive and then to sales manager there.

After the IPO, she took a position as head of sales at a small startup for two years. This new company was a completely different kind of animal. A chicken maybe? He hadn't heard of it. From what he could find in the many articles online, it seemed they had decent technology and great founders, but no traction. Like a chicken—a lot of flapping, but it just couldn't get off the ground.

From there, she landed at GigaTech five years ago. That would have been a few years after their massive IPO at an $11 billion valuation. She started as a director of sales, became regional vice president, and was presently the senior vice president of sales for North America. Now that was impressive. That was the kind of path Arlo imagined for himself. Perhaps he'd found the right person.

■ ■ ■

At exactly noon, Arlo stepped off the elevator on the forty-fifth floor of the GigaTech building and was greeted by a panoramic view of the city. It was jaw-dropping. *So this is the view from the top.* It was an open-floor plan with offices around the perimeter, floor-to-ceiling glass everywhere and gentle grey, powder blue, and white touches that matched the sky beyond—a truly heavenly impression.

One thing he knew about executives from his own experience was that their meetings never started on time. No sooner had he sat when Alex swung her head around a corner.

"There he is! You actually showed up!" she said with a wry smile, "That's a good start! Come on, Arlo." She swung back the other way, vanishing.

"Hi Alex." He chased after her, extending a hand, which she missed. "Thanks for meeting." It was an awkward attempt at formalizing the conversation. Something about the view, the cacophony of activity on the floor behind her, and her promptness seemed to command formality.

"The entire floor is the sales team." She gestured to a huge contingent of fully-engaged salespeople with headsets on, two monitors at each workstation. Some stood at standing desks, some reclined and looked out of the windows while in conversation, some collaborated in small conference rooms.

It was alive! The energy was contagious.

The screens overlooking the sales floor showed speedometer-style dashboards—all pinned in the green—as an indication of goals being crushed. Anyone who happened to catch his eye managed to offer a quick smile without missing a beat in their workflow.

Alex led him across the open floor to a corner, where her sparse office sat perched over one of the busiest intersections in the city down below. She offered him a seat at a large, round, glass table with four chic chairs and remained standing, taking in the scene below.

He knew that she was probably very busy, and he had rehearsed his part. His pitch. He wanted to make the most of her time.

He quickly got to the point. "My team consists of sales reps who are eager to succeed and I am struggling to grow them and maximize their effectiveness. I'm worried about keeping the good ones if we aren't successful as a team. I have studied discovery skills, demos, proposal presentation, conversion metrics, activity volume, and prospecting. I listen to calls, review e-mails, and consistently create an atmosphere of high motivation. We do short competitions religiously. But something is missing. I don't feel I have a handle on the things that matter. I don't think that I am driving each individual to their greatest success or motivating them enough. There must be something more." He paused to take a breath.

"Well, that's a mouthful, Arlo. I'm not sure you said much though." Alex paused and gazed out of the window in silence for what seemed like a long time.

"Whether in sports or the arts, personally or professionally, the term 'coach' is used to identify an individual who elevates the performance of another. That is a mighty lofty ambition. Wouldn't you say?" she said.

He agreed.

"An athletic coach typically has spent years in his or her given sport. A vocal coach may have produced beautiful music. A personal coach has typically spent years in either study or in contemplation of the things that make humans tick. Each is granted episodic interactions with the person they are coaching—daily or weekly or even less frequently, which culminate in a performance, or may even endure over a lifetime.

"The same isn't true in sales. In sales, companies typically promote a high performer to their level of incompetence, slap them on the back, and say good luck! You've heard of the Peter Principle?"

Arlo swallowed hard on hearing another foreign concept that Alex was sharing. "No, I haven't . . ."

She walked over to a tall, white bookshelf, which was surprisingly disorganized for such a minimalist office. Half-opened books lay on top of books with yellow sticky notes protruding from their edges. The corner of the bottom shelf, barely visible from where he sat, looked to hold a cluttered pile of glass awards and ribbons bearing the GigaTech symbol. Accomplishments cast aside by someone who seemingly had more important things to focus on.

She grabbed a book titled *The Peter Principle: Why Things Always Go Wrong* and read from a dog-eared page, "Given enough time—and assuming the existence of enough ranks in the hierarchy—each employee rises to, and remains at, his level of incompetence." Alex paused for dramatic effect, locking eyes with Arlo who wondered if this assertion was directed at him specifically. It could explain some of the imposter syndrome he regularly felt.

"Provided with no frameworks and little direction, it is no surprise that newly-minted managers seldom evolve into good coaches," Alex said. "It happened to me too. I climbed the rungs of sales management through talent, drive, and repeating a process I had stitched together over the years. I had some unconscious competence, but without specifically learning how to coach, my results were inconsistent, and my teams seldom became more than a collection of a few high performers . . . and then the rest. That just doesn't get it done."

Arlo wondered if she was referring to the chicken—the company where Alex had been head of sales. It had all of this promise, and seemingly a great team, but never took off.

"Effective sales coaching can impact revenue more significantly than any other sales management activity. But there is too little time. Managers are always battling a fire or stretching to another target. In sales, we don't get timeouts, an offseason, training camp, or days between games. We don't get a ton of time to practice until we get it right."

This speech sounded familiar to Arlo as he mentally reviewed his own career path. There was a firehose process of onboarding into his first sales role, with a steadily increasing ramp to quota. From there, it was all fast-paced. He had been afforded training sessions for new product features. He attended sales kick-off workshops with outside trainers who came with their stories from other companies—some worn out jokes, anecdotes and movie references, slide decks full of tips and tricks, and half-baked theories with negligible lasting impact. But in reality, the bulk of his activity as a sales rep, and as a manager now, was focused on actual conversations.

Alex was back at the window. "Looking down from here, Arlo, it seems as though there is a randomness to the cars turning left and right. The people crossing streets. It looks like a beautiful orchestration of random acts performing somehow in unison. But, in fact . . ." she pushed her short hair behind her ear and cocked her head toward Arlo, gently tapping the window with her finger.

"Every single person down there, whether in a car or on foot, has free will and is influenced into making a conscious decision about where they are going. Maybe it's shopping, maybe it's work, maybe it's lunch, maybe it's home. But what looks to be pretty random from here becomes incredibly personal on the ground."

Arlo contemplated the reference and stole a glance at the gold clock on the bookshelf next to a basketball littered with autographs. He wasn't sure how much time he had with Alex, but he needed some answers.

"The same goes for coaching people. Right now, it probably seems as though you've put up some streetlights and crosswalks as guidance, and your team is randomly applying your training, process, and systems. Right?"

Arlo thought about it. "That's exactly what it seems like."

Alex crossed the room to her standing desk, which held only a laptop, a cell phone, her coffee cup from the morning, and a book wrapped in plastic, which she brought back to the table and placed before him.

Yes, yes, yes!!!! This is what I've been waiting for! He couldn't wait to tear into the book. He'd searched online and found nothing of this sort. *Where did she get it? How did she know they would be meeting?* A wave of relief washed over him and his leg began to bounce anxiously.

"Arlo, years ago, I was seeking too. I wanted to dramatically improve both my team and individual sales rep performance. I wanted to positively influence the lives of the individuals I am responsible to manage. I hated feeling like I had failed a sales rep and had to fire them because they couldn't meet expectations."

Arlo nodded, knowing that feeling all too well. Maximilian came to mind, specifically. While there is a chance he was a bad hire in the first place, his downward spiral was puzzling, and Arlo couldn't help but wonder if there was something more he should have done to give him a greater chance at success.

Alex went on, "You have to know what you are looking for to be able to find it. I had gotten to the end of my rope. The startup where I was head of sales had crashed and burned, and I'd just been offered a job here, at GigaTech. I was sure that all of these smart people here would figure out in short order that team building was not my strong suit." She laughed at the memory.

"They say, 'When the student is ready, the teacher will appear,' you know? Well, that's when I was introduced to the C.O.A.C.H. framework." She drifted back from that moment to the present with a soft, sincere gaze.

"I have found, quite frankly, coaching to be the most incredibly rewarding aspect of management. Sure, you can make a ton of money, win awards and accolades, and no one loves competition more than me. But I have shared the C.O.A.C.H. framework over the years with new sales managers like you, and some of the crustiest, seasoned professionals. I've shared it with individuals who don't manage anyone but have learned that they can coach *themselves* toward greater goals and ambitions." Her excitement was contagious.

"Our sales enablement team has used the C.O.A.C.H. framework to elevate their position into a more strategic partnership with me by impacting manager performance and not just focusing their attention on individual contributors. I've even taught the framework to consultants and advisors, who have improved the quality of their work with clients by both implementing and teaching the C.O.A.C.H. framework." Alex paused and leaned forward, elbows on the table.

"Almost weekly, I get a note from someone I've shared this framework with, thanking me for the impact it has had on their lives or their careers. Honestly? That's the best reward."

Arlo liked the sound of that. His teacher had appeared. He was ready.

"So, if you have been asking yourself why what I said in the coffee shop has been stuck in your head, I think that means that you were seeking answers too. Am I right?"

Arlo appreciated being asked the question. So often in his role he felt like he was supposed to magically have the answers, and questions were frowned upon. This sounded like just what he'd been looking for, but instead of relief, Arlo began to feel a deep pit in his stomach. The idea that there was a framework seemed perfectly logical, but he was worried about complexity and the time needed to learn yet another doggone sales methodology. So many of these things made sense in a classroom, in practice, he found that most training and "frameworks" were impractical. And he was running out of time.

"Yes. I'm ready. Yes!" he said.

6

WHY COACHING FAILS

*A salesperson cannot be effectively coached until you have
validated their skills.*

*A salesperson can only control the quality and quantity of
his or her activity. That's it.*

He already had doubts as to whether he'd be able to execute this
C.O.A.C.H. framework, but he hoped that if he got one or two
good tips, those might make a difference, save his quarter, and
save his career. It felt like a good plan. The only plan.

Alex stood. She wasn't one for sitting still. She crossed to the other
side of the office, picking up a stress ball en route. She tossed it from
hand to hand below a photo of Michael Jordan and the Chicago
Bulls. It wasn't a trophy presentation or a game highlight . . . It
looked like a snapshot from a post-practice huddle. Each player
was dripping sweat in their practice jerseys and surrounding Phil

Jackson. Of all the Bulls photos Arlo had seen, he had never seen this one before.

The white wall framed her in a short, yellow jacket, black-rimmed glasses, and those expensive jeans his ex-girlfriend had explained "aren't just jeans," when he had insisted that hundreds of dollars for a pair of jeans was absolutely ridiculous. He always thought those photos were carefully staged, but she looked ready for the cover of *Forbes*. It was clear that Alex was accustomed to owning the room.

"What makes managing salespeople harder than any other role in a company?" She tossed him the ball—literally and figuratively.

He missed the catch, but said, "Salespeople are self-directed. Their daily schedule is their own and it's primarily determined by the meetings they schedule with prospects in their pipeline and the effort they make trying to find new ones. Apart from internal meetings, they don't have much oversight."

He tried to draw the ball closer, with an outstretched foot, but ended up kicking it further away. "I also have salespeople in multiple locations. One works from home."

Pacing, she picked up the ball again. "Go on."

"They have half of their earnings tied to variable compensation based on specific performance metrics. Aligning that performance and activity to the things that drive the business can be challenging." Arlo paused, taking in how overwhelmed he had been in his role all this time. Not one to complain, he had kept most of these thoughts bottled inside and just showed up to do the job every day. But now that he'd voiced these challenges aloud, he felt a sense of doom. *How can I possibly overcome these things? They just exist. There's no solution to the structure of a sales team.* He sighed.

"That's a good start, Arlo" Alex said, tossing him the ball underhand and slowly, like one would to a toddler. He caught it this time.

"I have a few more challenges that fall into the self-inflicted category," she said. "First of all, I've seen managers fail at coaching because they create sliding targets in the form of continually adjusting a salesperson's quota, tools, territory, methodology, administrative responsibilities, and other day-to-day tasks. Managers wreak havoc, which results in team apathy and an inability to hold reps accountable." She peered over her glasses, probing for acknowledgement.

Arlo thought about his own organization and how, because of growth, leadership made similar decisions. He was left to deliver the news and attempt to manage a team that was often disoriented and scared. He knew that a good rep like Jackie would eventually quit, leaving him with a revenue gap and a seat to fill that would require a good chunk of his time and attention. He also realized that these quick switches contributed to Seth nodding his head in agreement but never changing his behavior. Why would he? Things would probably swing in another direction soon.

Alex continued, "Sometimes a new quarterly compensation plan gets rolled out mid-quarter but is not immediately finalized. As a result, what do you think happens to the sales team?"

Arlo knew this one well. "They don't know what their specific goals are or how they are going to be paid. So they just idle. More energy is invested in worrying about if they can pay their bills or looking at other opportunities than focusing on improving their selling skills. At my last company, every single person on the sales team had their own manual compensation calculator! Huge waste of effort."

Alex nodded. "That's right. People respond poorly when there is a lack of clarity. Productivity diminishes, or energy is spent in the wrong direction. Beyond compensation, how about the activity necessary to be successful as a salesperson? It can vary, right?" She was ticking things off on her fingers.

"Absolutely. From organization to organization." Arlo knew these things in spades. He may not have had answers, but he definitely understood the problems.

"Discovery calls, demos, executive presentations, proposals, prospecting, events and trade shows—there are tons of activities," he said.

"With varying impact. How often are these activities prescribed clearly by management?" Alex said. "It's not fair for a manager to expect sales reps to do things which they were not told to do, or in a manner different than what they were trained." She steadied her eyes, looking into the depths of Arlo's soul.

He knew precisely what she meant. There were times when he would throw up his hands privately, thinking: *What the hell are you doing? Why aren't you getting a clear commitment? Why aren't you disqualifying prospects that obviously don't have pain?* When, in fact, he had never given any specific instruction to do so. He had just hoped the sales rep would figure it out.

"Unclear expectations are really a symptom of irresponsible and inept management," she said emphatically, presenting her closing argument. He could not object.

"Then, there is the issue of consistency," Alex continued. She moved around the room as though her feet were connected to her thoughts. She tapped a finger on her pursed lips to gather the next one. "Inspect what you expect. You've heard that before, right?"

"Sure. It's not enough to let sales reps know what your expectations are. You have to then micromanage and be sure that things get done," Arlo said.

"Not micromanage, Arlo. No one wants to work for a micromanager," she said. "But you need a transparent system of record and a means by which a manager and sales rep can communicate based upon data, not narrative."

"Okay. Well, we use a CRM," Arlo said defensively.

"Sponge, not a rock, Arlo," she reminded him. "I'm on your side; any criticism is constructively intended. Soak it up. Good managers are good listeners and are able to compartmentalize their own emotions."

"Got it," Arlo said, meeting her eyes and straightening his spine.

"CRM is great technology. However, even with a CRM in place, few companies use the data properly to track, analyze, and have an ongoing dialogue about how a salesperson is tracking toward their goal. Instead, the CRM serves as the basis for a subjective narrative."

"Subjective narrative?" he asked.

"Yeah. Think about your team meetings." She returned to her chair, arms crossed on the table. He squeezed the stress ball in his lap. "Are they fairly repetitive measurements of specific events, probabilities, and clear next steps a prospect has agreed to take? Or are they, instead, colorful narratives about prospect conversations, what they are *thinking about*, actions the salesperson will *follow up* with?" she continued. "Or worse, just a guess at progress toward a goal?"

"I see what you're saying. I mean, there are times I am sitting in a one-on-one, listening to a sales rep tell me things which I am fairly certain are either embellishments or wishful thinking," Arlo agreed.

"Well, it's your fault. If you're not strictly talking about the data, then you are inviting your reps to 'Sales Story Time' and waiting for what you want to hear." There was that smile again. "Create an environment which uses data to evaluate facts and accepts the facts as the basis upon which strategy and tactics are deployed."

It made perfect sense. "Like the military?" he asked.

"Yes, like the military. But remember, your prospect is not the enemy. They are your partner. It is not an adversarial relationship," she explained. "A salesperson can only control the quality and quantity of his or her activity. That's it. They cannot control the outcome of that activity, so stop talking about outcomes. Focus on the things that can be controlled. The things a salesperson can choose to do. The mastery with which they are done."

Just then, Arlo realized that he had not brought his notebook. He looked apologetically around the room. "Could I please borrow a notepad?" She looked down at the book on the table and raised an eyebrow in confirmation as he tore the plastic off of the cover. *Finally! The unveiling!*

But it was empty. Save for a "Property Of:" page in the beginning of the book, it looked . . . to . . . be . . . empty. *What the hell? What am I supposed to study here?* It was an empty journal.

Alex sensed his disappointment and laughed out loud. "Oh, you thought I was going to just hand you . . ." Her hands fell to her knees as she bent down, and her hair covered her face as she burst into hysterical laughter. "Sorry. Is that how you coach your people? Just give them tools and a slap on the back? No wonder they're gonna fire you." *Ouch*. He really didn't need the reminder. He found the first empty page as she handed him a pen, and he began to make notes.

"Focus on the things that they can control," he repeated. "The things a salesperson can choose to do and the mastery with which they are done. Got it."

"Do you?" she asked, skeptically.

"Sure. That makes sense. You cannot control the prospect, but you can control yourself. So ensure that the actions you are taking are consistent with the things that have worked in the past, and that you are executing them in the most effective way," he said.

"Precisely. Just how do you go about doing that across an entire team?" she said, rising from her chair again and moving over to the glass windows.

"What do you mean?" he said.

"Well, one of the challenges of management is that it involves *other people*." She laughed and tapped the window, reminding Arlo of the random, not-random activity down below. "Your response would work well if you only had to apply it to your own sales activity. Because *you* have achieved a certain level of competence. But the challenge in management is that you've got to execute that concept across varying levels of aptitude, experience, and competence."

"Right." Arlo remembered how difficult it could be to get consistent performance from his team on something as seemingly simple as asking a pain-based discovery question in the first five minutes of a discovery call. *I mean how hard is that?* "So, how do you do that?"

"Frameworks, Arlo! Frameworks!" She raised a pointed finger to the sky. "Managers wear so many hats and have so many things to do that coaching will be dead last, or just won't happen if there's no way to make it both effective and efficient. But you know what else?"

"What else?" Arlo played along.

Alex returned to the table, voice hushed in a conspiratorial tone. "If a company does not have a clear, trained, and rigorously applied sales methodology, then a manager becomes a constant, ad hoc trainer which is exhausting and unrealistic. Then you simply can't coach, because a salesperson cannot be expected to respond to coaching if they haven't been trained." She paused, looking at the journal, indicating that he should write that down.

"Salespeople cannot be expected to respond to coaching if they haven't been trained," he repeated, writing. "So if I am not using a clear sales methodology or clear sales frameworks . . ."

"Then your sales people will default to what is comfortable, and you can't hold them accountable to anything otherwise," she finished. "Then you cannot effectively coach, because everyone will be doing something different. It's chaos. Ever watched a pickup game of basketball versus a team that's been coached?" He knew exactly what she meant.

Arlo thought about the fits and starts his company had with different sales methodologies. Leadership would roll something out, have a consultant train it, then make no further efforts toward reinforcement or accountability. As if the team would retain a wholly new system through osmosis.

Though he had only been at VizuData for six months, some on his team had been trained in three different methodologies in two years. Methodology might even be a generous term. A new hire like Lindsay had only been trained on the product and received a few slide decks and videos about an acronym for qualifying.

"So then what happens is that managers manufacture ways to be relevant to their team. This actually erodes the relationship. Like coming to one-on-one meetings asking a bunch of questions which could easily have been answered by the CRM, just trying to get in face time, but providing no value whatsoever to the sales rep. Huge morale killer!" She slapped the table with an open hand, her diamond ring clanging hard against the glass.

"Couple that with zero follow-through. If you're making it up as you go along, there is no way a coaching conversation can maintain momentum from one meeting to the next. So, salespeople just check out at some point. What's the point if there's no value?"

Arlo flashed back to the countless, well-intentioned, one-on-one conversations he'd had with sales reps. Action items agreed upon. But then he never closed the loop. Never went back to review results. So Seth kept doing the same thing, Derek floundered in the weeds, Samantha stayed under the radar, Lindsay maintained the status quo, and Maximillian bowed out.

Jackie performed in spite of him. Not because of him.

"Coaching conversations are not events. They are threads. They should have continuity," Alex said. "Stitching one to the next and creating a body of work."

"Like a quilt" Arlo said, remembering his grandmother's patch-work quilts. Though each square was distinct, they were uniform in size and shape and came together to form a whole.

"Right. Like a quilt," Alex said. "Each coaching session should be a continuation of the last and must build upon the successes or challenges specific to the individual and their ability to support the goals of the business. Salespeople will be rigorously engaged if each session is an additional step toward their personal and professional development. And ultimately, there should be evidence of the effort they have made."

"So then, you are saying that it's my responsibility to stitch this all together? For each salesperson? That's a lot of quilting!" he said.

"Well, coaching is often misconstrued, actually," Alex said.

Arlo furrowed his brow and cocked his head. "How so?"

"For one, many managers believe that coaching is purely a punitive exercise," she said, searching for signs of understanding. "What I mean is that many managers only coach problems. Instead of reinforcing excellence. You know what that does?"

Arlo knew so exactly. In fact, he had worked for a manager early in his career who seemed to go out of his way to identify things each rep needed to fix. No one on the team was ever rewarded or encouraged for successes. It began to feel mean-spirited even, and had destroyed the culture of the team, leading to high turnover and a lot of good people leaving.

He, on the other hand, had gone out of his way to ensure that he was not too critical of his team, which actually left him feeling handcuffed at times.

His head was spinning, thinking of the fact that he poked holes in Jackie's work instead of building on the positives, even though she was the most consistent person on the team, and her only issues were minor things directly related to the fact that she was junior.

"Absolutely. It ruins morale. But how do you strike a balance between offering critical feedback and not being punitive?" he asked.

"Now you're asking good questions. Write that one down," she said. "A second false belief is that coaching is training," she continued. "A salesperson cannot be effectively coached until you have validated their skills."

"What exactly does that mean? Validated their skills?"

"Well, suppose I give you a little guidance on performing brain surgery? Then you get down to General Hospital and help out a patient. Would that be okay?" she said.

Arlo laughed. "Yeah, sure! Don't think it will help much though. And I'm not sure anyone would want to go under my knife."

"Why not? I can give you a few tips, and you can cruise around social media to see if you can find a few more . . ."

"Okay, I get it. No matter how much coaching you or an actual brain surgeon were to offer me—I'd be no better at the job. Because I haven't been trained in brain surgery," he said.

"Makes a lot of sense when we are talking about brain surgery, right? Now, fair enough, sales is neither rocket science nor brain surgery. But it's not easy, and it is, in fact, science," she said. This was one of those statements that remained in the air like a refreshing mist.

"So, if I am coaching someone on discovery, but I have not fully trained them on how to uncover pain, then what you're saying is that I'm not actually helping," Arlo said.

"If you were a basketball coach trying to get a team to run the Triangle offense, but they haven't even been trained on and proven their ability to run a three-man-weave, how effective do you think they are gonna be?" she asked.

He half expected her to take a knee with a clipboard in hand and start sketching Xs and Os. The reference was a little dated, he thought, but point taken.

Alex, as if reading his mind, continued, "The Triangle would still reign supreme with a team smart enough to read and react and execute precision cuts." He had nothing to say, no argument to make.

Alrighty then. "So then, training equips people with the knowledge they need to do the job. That's not coaching," Arlo concluded.

"Coaching allows them to apply that knowledge with ever-increasing impact," she said. She nodded at his notebook.

He wrote it down. "And a salesperson cannot be effectively coached until their skillset has been validated or trained."

"Now we're getting somewhere." Alex clapped her hands and glanced at her watch. "So, we don't have a ton of time left today. This week, I'm going to introduce you to some of my managers who are going to give you a crash course on how we coach. But first, you need to understand the psychological drivers that make it work."

"The psychological drivers?" This was getting interesting.

7

THE FIRST FRAMEWORK: S.C.A.L.E.

When I become aware that any S.C.A.L.E. driver has been impacted negatively, I just work to ensure that I am maximizing its reward instead of creating a threat perception.

Arlo leaned forward in his chair and turned another page in his new notebook. He glanced at the simple gold clock on Alex's bookshelf. Twelve-thirty. He couldn't help but realize that he had learned more about management in the last thirty minutes than he had in the last six months.

How do managers typically learn these things? Do you just have to hope that you end up working for someone who knows? How could Gabe have expected him to be successful all this time just by "figuring it out"?

While so far this meeting with Alex had been illuminating, there was also this deep sense of unease. What else was he missing? How far did he have to go?

"Arlo, are you still with me?" Alex asked, seeing him shift in his seat. She was ready to push forward.

"Yes, the drivers."

"Your five best friends," she said. "You are going to need these friends because the role of a salesperson can feel like a roller-coaster ride. It can be emotionally and even physically draining, so any team will needs a lot of feedback and motivation.

Alex paused briefly for dramatic effect, making sure that the point sank in.

"This is one of the reasons why so few managers are consistently effective coaches. It can be exhausting, week after unforgiving week, to keep your team whole, motivated, and focused on the activity necessary to be successful."

"Sometimes I wonder why it seems so hard to just be consistent," he said.

"Did you know you have the responsibility, as a manager, to ensure that you have created an environment which is receptive to your coaching activity?" Alex asked.

"Receptive? I'm their boss. Isn't that enough?" he said, half laughing.

Alex laughed too. "You would think so, right? But that's not how human beings work. We're motivated by many things, authority being one of the least. And before you say it—money isn't the top motivator either."

"Maybe that's why the spiffs I roll out at the end of each quarter do very little to move the needle on the numbers," he said.

"Could be. Receptivity to coaching is essential. How can you coach someone who is unwilling to be open and honest with you?" she said. "Think of our first conversation. How would we be speaking now if you had told me some garbage about how you were behind your number, but *felt good about hitting your goal* and had *confidence in your pipeline coverage*, blah blah," she said, rolling her eyes and mimicking a sock puppet with her hand.

Arlo laughed because she sounded like some of his sales reps. In fact, he had just had a meeting with Derek about his pipeline, but he felt as though Derek had just told him what he thought he wanted to hear instead of the truth. "Right. It's hard to coach without trust."

"Exactly!" She jumped up and walked over to the bookshelf. He gazed outside as a cloud covered the building. "Do you know what this is?" She picked up an object on the bookshelf. It was an old, rusty scale. Not like the scales of justice. Just a simple metal scale like his great grandmother may have used to weigh food.

"Uh . . . it looks like a scale?" he said.

"That's correct. Why do you think I have an old scale in my office?" Alex said as she sat on the table in front of him.

Arlo got that uncomfortable feeling again. *Man, she asks a lot of weird questions.* He thought back to his ex-girlfriend who was always making him try a cleansing of some sort or a superfood juice or a new energy diet. "Are you doing a paleo . . .?"

She cut him off. "Oh please. You think I would waste my time with you on a diet rant?" Then to herself, "This is going to be tougher than I thought."

She was still smiling. He was beginning to realize that she said everything with a slight smile. He was reminded how someone had once told him that you can say anything in the South as long as it's followed by, "Bless his heart." *This little simpleton thinks the key to sales coaching is in a smoothie . . . bless his heart.*

"It is a scale. Because S.C.A.L.E.[1] is actually an acronym for the fundamentals of human behavioral drivers. If I am constantly mindful of these drivers in all of my interactions, then I create opportunities to positively impact behavior. Receptivity to coaching," she explained. Her pace quickened, inviting him to come along for the journey.

"Wow," he said and immediately wished he had mustered a more thoughtful response.

"Yes! Wow!" she said, nodding in agreement. "Follow me here. The acronym S.C.A.L.E. stands for Status, Certainty, Autonomy, Likeness, and Equity." She moved to the whiteboard and, in terrible, hasty handwriting, began to scrawl the letters in earnest.

"I am a big fan of acronyms," she said.

"They are easy to remember," Arlo offered.

"Yes they are. That's the primary reason I use them," she said. "They also allow me to convey a large amount of knowledge quickly, ensure that my managers execute competently, and that we are all communicating clearly and efficiently."

That sounded impressive. Arlo thought about his own management team meetings. It sometimes felt as though each manager had their own language. Some would say that deals were "warm", others liked colors and would say, "This one is in the red zone," and still others would conjure percentages—"60 percent probability." He wasn't sure if one knew what the other was talking about, but no one dug deeper. It was more about reporting out—and getting out!

"Human interaction is always subject to the interpretation of the individuals involved. So I needed a way to keep my managers aligned to the things that we can measure which relate to basic human drivers. It's challenging, if not impossible, for co-workers to communicate effectively when discussing complex conversations if there isn't a common language.

"In the last ten years, there have been advances in neuroscience which have demystified these human drivers. Problem is, most managers are so busy with numbers that they haven't spent much time on the psychology. Neuroscience is not the first place sales managers go to when trying to identify how to hit revenue goals!" Alex shrugged her shoulders and rolled her eyes, laughing at herself.

"No. I can't say that I've been spending my nights on neuroscience podcasts," he agreed. *Note to self: Listen to neuroscience podcasts.*

"Of course not. And you don't need to. But you need to understand some basic themes. That's why I use the S.C.A.L.E. framework. It makes it easy for my team." She had written the word "Status" on the whiteboard.

"Status is our perception of where we stand in relation to our peers. Scientists have observed that when we perceive a drop in our Status, our brain networks light up in the same way as if we have experienced actual physical pain! How incredible is that?" Her eyes lit up, and her pace was quickening again. "It's like we've been physically harmed. Have you ever been embarrassed?"

"Of course I have." Arlo was thinking of the time he accidentally spilled red wine on the white rug at his boss's house. "It sucks."

"Yeah, it does." She nodded emphatically. "How did you feel in the moment?"

"I felt low. Like everyone was looking at me, and I didn't measure up. It still stings," he said.

"Stings! Yes! Perfect word. That's how people describe a negative impact on status. Words like 'sting' or 'slap in the face.' Have you ever wondered why we use physical descriptors?"

Arlo thought about it a bit. "Because it actually hurts?" He considered this and marveled at the revelation.

"Conversely, as our perception of status increases, we feel safe. A perceived increase in Status actually lights up neurological networks more significantly than when we receive a monetary reward." She paused. "Can you think of a time when you felt an increase in Status?"

He thought about the first time he'd topped the leaderboard in revenue as an account executive, despite being the youngest person on the team and it only being his second quarter in the role. He had felt safe. While the money was great, what he really loved was the feeling of being top dog on the sales floor, and all of the respect that came along with it.

"Yeah, I know the exact feeling you're describing. Is that why management books suggest praising in public and reprimanding in private?" he said.

"Got that right. So as managers, we have to keep in mind that status is a driver for our sales reps. When events, or worse, when we as coaches damage it, we lose trust and impact. For instance, good coaches always use questions to navigate coaching conversations rather than just making statements or declarations."

"How do you mean?"

"Well, Arlo, given what I've told you about status, tell me a situation with a sales rep where you think this driver may have been at work," she asked.

Arlo thought about it and it hit him. "Seth has struggled in making the transition from doing community work, where he was a superstar at getting signatures and knocking on doors. He has said that he felt like a fish out of water. He's not converting conversations well because he's trying to get people interested instead of finding problems he can solve." It was as though Arlo was seeing Seth clearly for the first time. "He doesn't feel respected by the team. I should be more aware that the transition is probably contributing to his level of frustration and disengagement from the group."

"What do you mean by 'be more aware'?"

"I can help ease the transition by reminding him of the tools he used to be successful in in his previous role, reinforcing those, and helping him understand that it's normal to find the transition challenging, and tell him that I hired him because of his potential."

Alex lifted her eyebrows and smiled. "See?"

"See what?" he said. He sensed that something profound had just occurred by the satisfaction he saw on Alex's face.

"If I had said, 'You probably have people on your team who are struggling with Status right now. That's something you should fix.' How would you have responded?"

He thought about it. "Probably defensively. It would have felt like an attack."

"Why?"

"Ahhh . . . because it would have affected my status," he said as Alex steepled her hands together.

"That's right. It would have been perceived as a threat. Our job as managers is to minimize threats and maximize rewards. It's critical that we are mindful of each individual's status. Not our own—but that of each individual we manage. I asked you a simple and unbiased question, and you were able to evaluate your own performance, and I can provide supportive feedback."

Arlo captured this in his notebook. "Right."

Alex wrote "Certainty" on the board.

"Certainty. Ambiguity of any kind is also perceived as a threat to human beings. We are always trying to predict what is going to happen next," she said. "Right now, your brain is asking 'What will she say next? How much time do we have left? When can I eat lunch? How does this all come together?'"

Arlo laughed. "That's pretty dead-on."

"It's a survival mechanism from when we lived in caves. If we weren't always anticipating, then it would be hard to ensure that our core needs were met every day. That instinct doesn't just go away because we have grocery stores and paychecks," she said. "When we, as managers provide clear expectations, we allay fear and build confidence."

"Like when you told me to come at noon, with a notebook, and to be a sponge—not a rock!" he said.

"Precisely. If I had not mentioned to you that the goal was for you to just soak things up, you may have misunderstood, and felt that I was testing you. Or felt that you had to prove something. Or that it was your job to just to pick my brain," she said. "None of which are roles that would have been very receptive to coaching, am I right?"

Arlo agreed. "It would have been a lot more difficult to focus." He paused. "Wow. So, when you talked about changing compensation mid-quarter, this is what you were referring to? And the same could be true for changing other things like messaging or introducing new products. There are a lot of variables in a sales-person's world—some that cannot be controlled . . . like how a prospect responds. But for those that can be controlled, I have to create certainty around expectations."

"One way I like to do this is to break down the complex into smaller bits. It's important to have huge goals and objectives—those are the vision of your company. Then, it is the role of the manager to take those and reduce them to the bits which can be made certain, acted upon, and measured every day," she said. "Ironically, the ability to do this creates a higher tolerance for uncertainty."

"Because you can take the uncertain and reduce it to what you can control now," Arlo offered.

"You've just stated a pretty darned good thesis for the selling profession there, Arlo! I like that. So to maximize the reward of certainty you have to remember that the human brain prefers the predictable. It makes us feel safe. Be clear in your expectations and provide feedback to acknowledge progress, no matter how audacious a goal or objective may be."

"Understood." He was definitely going to need a larger notebook. He anticipated a few tips and tricks, but this was turning into a master class.

Next Alex wrote "Autonomy."

"Any guesses on this one?" she said.

"Sure. Human beings like to do things on their own. We like freedom of choice. So I can't box people in or be too rigorous," he said, framing the statement with his hands.

"You're going in the right direction," she said. "Yes. As human beings, we like to use our own initiative. You must create space for this for the members of your team. Whether that's designing their own schedule, the tools, or frequency, or channels they will use to hit their goal, messaging options that have been proven . . . You notice that all of these are things which are still certain, however."

"Okay, so then, rigorous, but not dogmatic?" He raised an eyebrow.

"Sure. We can go with that. In other words, you want to tee up your folks for success. You still have to manage them effectively—and with some synergy—or you won't have impactful data points. But getting too involved in the day-to-day operations is micromanagement. That will exhaust you and build resentment on both sides."

"I have to show that I trust their judgement and their commitment."

"That's right. So if you create some certainty around expectations, and have validated the effectiveness of the activities they are doing, you can provide autonomy by allowing salespeople to take on more responsibility and to experiment with new ideas."

Arlo shriveled his nose a bit at the concept of his salespeople experimenting. He'd seen how that turned out. Wasted weeks of bad messaging, misused technology, or ineffective demos. At the top of his mind was the last experiment that Maximilian had run before he was fired, where he'd wanted to test e-mail messaging by persona type. He'd sent six e-mails at once to every persona.

Alex picked up on his resistance.

"I used the term experiment purposely," she said. "I didn't say 'play around with' or 'try out.' Experimentation is a scientific process. We do it with tools, messaging, content—everything. The evaluation is done alongside a control, a system which we know to provide consistent results. Then we measure. If our hypothesis is right, we plan to integrate the new system. If not, it's scrapped with little impact on what is already successful."

That sounded a whole lot different than the wholesale messaging changes his team seemed to swing from like a pendulum every sixty days.

"So there is a system, or structure," he created rails with his hands on the table, "and inside of that a salesperson can run experiments which allow for autonomy."

"Sure. Just like a team sport. Whether on offense or defense, the team has practiced and perfected specific plays. Inside of those plays, there are a number of variations allowed for each role, subject to the variables encountered by the individual."

"So again," Arlo picked up on the thought, "it's critical that the team is trained on both the fundamentals and on the plays . . ."

"Or the whole thing is just chaos," Arlo concluded.

"Worse than the chaos," she said. "Managers will vacillate between delegation and micromanagement—setting the individual up for failure. The first time this happens will create a threat response in an individual. So instead, we maximize the opportunity for reward with this driver by ensuring that the system exists, training has been provided, competency validated, and then we can delegate and encourage autonomy within the system."

Arlo was writing in his notebook again and was beginning to understand the interdependence of all of these elements. He still wasn't sure how this would make him a better coach, but he was definitely beginning to understand that there was more to managing a team than the metrics and quantifying activity.

"The goal as a coach is to ensure that you are rising the tide of the team. By using autonomy wisely, you are enabling folks to demonstrate responsibility, initiative, and creativity. Don't ever be fooled into thinking that management has all the good ideas. I blew it big time with that idea."

"You did?" He found it hard to believe that Alex had ever struggled with these concepts.

"You bet. I failed miserably just before coming to GigaTech. In fact, I think it's one of the reasons they hired me. I was pretty candid about it, and executive management agreed that it was a great learning experience, but they also had a strong belief that the best managers understood that failure is part of the process of growth," she said.

"What were you doing wrong?" Arlo was intrigued.

"A laundry list of things!" she said, squeezing her forehead. "I thought that running hybrid sales methodologies at once was a good idea. I got creative with junk that I found on the internet because I wanted quick fixes instead of solutions. I hired on instinct instead of on data. I set goals without any attention to the sales math necessary to make them happen at each stage. Oh, I've got plenty of warts, Arlo! But specifically related to autonomy, I thought that I needed to be both the fuel and engine."

"The fuel and the engine?" Again he had no idea what she was talking about.

"Meaning, I would comb through posts online, read books, talk to peers, attend conferences, and come back with all of these 'ideas' about how to do things. Then I would present them in meetings with really rigorous activity associated with them." She was pacing and staring at the floor now with that look people get when they are trying to remember where they put something. "And the team would stare at me blank-faced."

Arlo wasn't too sure what the problem was here. It sounded like she had a team that wasn't too bright or just wasn't engaged.

"I would be seething inside because I had put all this work in, and they didn't seem to get onboard," she said. "But later, I found out what was really happening was that the team had come to realize that I had no interest in their input or feedback. I would go off and create in a black box and then present. They were not brought into to the process. What's worse is that my creative endeavors never really worked. So I lost their confidence."

A flicker of recognition crossed Arlo's face. *Is this why I get blank stares or gentle nods, but no change in behavior?*

"Yeah, it sucked," she said.

"So wait, then how did you go about fixing it?"

"Oh that was easy." She paused for dramatic effect. "I got fired." Not the answer Arlo was expecting. "Best think that ever happened to me, because I was in denial and thought that just because I was a pretty darned good salesperson, I could wing it on the management side. Wrong."

Alex let that linger in the air as she crossed back toward the whiteboard and wrote "Likeness."

"Any ideas?" she asked.

Arlo sighed aloud, driven back to the reason he was here. All of this was interesting, but, ultimately, if he wasn't able to get his team on track, he too would be fired.

"Well, I know that in the sales process, I've been taught that it's important to demonstrate *likeness* in order to establish rapport," he said.

"Okay. So what does that mean exactly?"

"I think it means that people buy from people they like. So, in order to coach effectively, I need to be liked, right?" he said.

Alex grimaced. "No, no, no. Do you think everyone liked Pat Riley? Bill Belichick? Pat Summit? How about Jack Welch? Carly Fiorina? Steve Jobs?" She pursed her lips, shaking her head.

"Probably not."

"Were they great coaches? Damned right they were." The side of her fist hit the whiteboard under the word "Likeness," startling Arlo. "Because they understood these principles Likeness is not likability. It's the fourth component of the S.C.A.L.E. framework and represents the ability to demonstrate relevance."

Arlo was confused. All this time he'd thought that prospects bought from him because he was likable. Because they liked him.

He had carried over this concept to his management role. *If they like me, they will respect me and they will follow me.* There had to be some truth to that.

"But, who accepts coaching from people they don't like?" he said.

She steadied her gaze. Enough so that it made it hard for him to swallow. "Do you like me, Arlo?" she said.

He gulped and immediately regretted it. "Do I like you?" *Stalling for time.*

"Yeah. Stop stalling. Do you like me?" she said.

He hadn't really thought about it. He was way more focused on trying to solve his coaching problem than making friends. "I mean, sure. You seem . . ."

"Oh please! You don't know or care if I am likable or not." She laughed. "And you shouldn't. Frankly, I'm not sure I like you, and I couldn't care less if you like me!"

Geez! That was harsh! But she was right. "I guess what I mean is that liking you is not part of the equation. You're . . ." the lightbulb went off, "coaching me." Arlo's chin dropped to his chest and he looked at his notebook as the point set in.

"Yes, I am." She was satisfied that he'd got the point. "Shall we continue?"

He nodded.

"Another mechanism that keeps us safe is the natural tendency to cast things that are new as a threat. We naturally feel initial discomfort. Think about when you go to a party where you don't know that many people," she said. "What initially goes through your mind as you enter the door?"

Arlo was pretty adept at social interactions, but mostly because he had learned to overcome that rush of anxiety that occurs initially upon entering a room filled with people he didn't know.

"I get that rush. My heart beats faster. Sometimes my palms sweat. I look around for someone I know or a friendly face."

"Once you've found that someone, what happens?" she asked.

"Well, then I feel like I'm on common ground. Sometimes it's just a greeting or a smile. If I don't get it pretty quickly, I'll engage with someone to strike up a conversation in the hope of finding something in common," he said.

"Otherwise?" she prodded.

"Otherwise, it's that uncomfortable thing of having my guard up and finding some corner to watch the room from without engaging," he said.

"That is typical human behavior," she said. "Did you hear yourself? You find a corner to watch from. That's instinctive. Suppose

I told you that the same issues are at play in developing relationships with members of your team."

Arlo literally moved to the edge of his seat.

"If we are conditioned to perceive anything unfamiliar as a threat, then that will create initial discomfort. If we are not offered some indication of likeness to us, then what do we do?"

"We move away from it! We don't engage." *Wow! I had no idea!* "So I need to make concepts relevant to my team in order for them to engage!"

"Not only relevant. You have to put them in context. That is what creates likeness. It's not just about explaining a concept; it's creating the hooks that make the individual see themselves. Do you do this with prospects?"

Arlo knew where she was going now. "You mean customer stories?"

"You got it," she said.

"We use them all the time in order to uncover pain, in order to frame the business case for a solution, even in uncovering resources to solve the problem." He had led countless trainings on the use of customer stories in the sales process.

"So, how often are you using stories in your coaching conversations?" she asked.

He couldn't think of a single time! His coaching conversations primarily centered around a point solution to resolving a problem he had identified—like not setting next steps, not uncovering real pain, or even not doing the activity.

"I don't think that I do. How would I incorporate a story in a coaching conversation?" Before he finished the sentence, he'd already got the answer. Alex had just done so when she'd shared her story about getting fired. *Damn, she's good.* "Forget it. Understood."

Alex tapped her forefinger to her temple as if to say "you're getting it."

"So we reduce threats and maximize rewards by creating likeness in the form of familiarity and context. Not by being fun, joining happy hour, or avoiding difficult conversations in order to be . . . liked," she said.

Yes. He would definitely need another notebook. "Why did you choose to share a story with me about your failure? You could have shared with me how you overcame the issue," he asked.

"I'm glad you asked," she said. "There are three reasons. First, the Likeness and commonality in this situation is entirely related to the problem. So, sharing how I overcame it does not increase our rapport or your receptivity to coaching. Instead, it further illuminates the gap." Her hands measured some distance between them. "I want you to feel, in the story that I share, that I am sitting beside you." She moved her chair next to his and sat down. "Now we are in this together and I can take you with me down a path I have a traveled. I can't just expect you to take that journey on your own. You don't have enough Certainty.

"Second, it's important that you understand the value of a mistake. You won't be willing to make them if you think that I view them as weakness or incompetence. So I am demonstrating my own vulnerability so that you can follow suit as we work together," she said. "Not to mention, frankly, that our mistakes always stand out more in memory than our successes. Think of when you learned to ride a bike."

Arlo thought back to his mother holding the back of his seat as he wobbled around the blacktop at a park near the house where he grew up. His feet alternately touched the ground as he tried to balance while keeping both hands on the handlebars.

"Did you fall?" she asked.

He remembered making a big circle, then realizing that his mother's voice was no longer right behind him—which made it impossible for her to still be holding the bike. He turned a sharp left—and flipped over the handlebars onto his shoulder, shrieking in pain as his mom crossed the playground at full speed.

"Yeah, I almost fell on my face. I remember it like it was yesterday. Then my mom made me get right back on the bike again." This time, he had made a mental note not to make sharp turns. A few more escorted laps and it had all clicked in.

"Do you remember the moment it all clicked?" she asked.

"Not really," he said. He was still reliving the fall as he crossed his arm to his shoulder.

"That's because we learn more from our mistakes than we do from our successes. They are seared into our memory and very easy to recall. So it's important that we acknowledge and invest energy in understanding them, or we'll make them again."

"Okay. That makes sense."

"Finally, I have come to learn that no one wants to hear about how great I am. Well, my mom likes that conversation, but no one I manage really cares." She waved her hand dismissively. "When I share how I have really screwed things up? Folks are all ears! It also keeps me grounded and authentic. I can't share stories I don't own. By owning my mistakes, it allows me to continue to grow."

Arlo took comfort in the fact that she had made plenty of mistakes. In fact, he had been feeling as though his mistakes were something to be hidden, lest his team feel he was unqualified for his position. It would be really empowering to drop that facade and instead share some of the challenges he'd faced when he was in their role, maybe even challenges he continued to face.

"I can easily see how this would create an environment that is more engaging. Also, I'm sick of pretending to be this flawless person. It feels like unnecessary pressure, and I don't think anyone's buying it anyway," he said.

"Trust me, they're not." She spun around and wrote "Equity" on the board. "Okay, last concept for today."

"Equity. This must mean the give and take." He dove in without waiting for the question to be asked. "A fair exchange."

"Exactly," she said, her forefinger touching her nose like in Charades. "You hit it on the head. But what exactly is being fairly exchanged."

"I would guess a number of things—goals, activity, compensation?" he said.

"There's no exchange in that statement, Arlo," she said. "Those are all measurements. Your definition was great but your example is very one-sided." She smiled.

"Equitable exchange means that each side is receiving something, right?" she said, and he raised his pen to his lips, considering her suggestion. "Inequitable exchange triggers a threat response in human beings. We don't like to be taken advantage of. The obvious examples are a con or a clear abuse of power. But I'll give you a less obvious example.

"Ever notice how sometimes, when you say hello to the cashier at the coffee shop downstairs and she'll smile and say hi back? Then there are times when he completely ignores you? That drives me frickin' crazy!" She balled both fists, shaking them back and forth. "What the hell is that?"

Arlo had to laugh. He had noticed. So he had stopped saying hello altogether. "I don't know! It's not even tied to how busy it is in there. It feels completely random."

"Completely random! Well . . . it's also unfair. This is a trivial example, but once we have offered something and it is not reciprocated, it impacts the equity driver so that we view it as an unfair exchange," she said. "This goes all the way back to the survival instinct as well. Fairness was an evolutionary advantage. Those of us who could detect deception in others or not fall victim to repeated broken promises or get scammed out of our share of the hunt were able to survive."

"So then, even a management relationship to a sales rep cannot be one-sided or authoritarian. Because the rep will not respond." He thought of the grousing that would take place when he just gave explicit direction (which had usually rolled downhill from leadership). It damaged morale and did nothing to increase productivity.

"And in the coaching relationship, it's a two-way street. The coach is responsible for availability, clarity, guidance, and follow-through. That is the exchange."

"So if I am asking someone to change a behavior, I have to make myself available for the conversation, provide clarity around the issue, be able to guide them on a path toward success, then follow through to be sure that it's being followed!" He felt like he was in *the zone*. It all made sense. He smiled a self-satisfied grin of understanding. He was writing frantically in his notebook now. Finger in air, "Hold that thought!"

Alex smiled back. Her glance was one of approval. Maybe a bit of relief that Arlo was finally putting it all together.

"Okay, so these are the S.C.A.L.E. drivers. I can measure my level of rapport with each member of my team based upon these basic human drivers. When I become aware that any S.C.A.L.E. driver has been impacted negatively, I just work to ensure that I am maximizing its reward instead of creating a threat perception.

"In advance of decision-making, I consider the impact of S.C.A.L.E. drivers on the team. Before a coaching conversation too. In fact, it's something I am constantly considering," she said. "When I speak to my managers about how they are managing their teams I always debrief on S.C.A.L.E. when they are experiencing a challenge with an individual."

Arlo leaned back, tapping his pen to his lips. "That's it?"

Alex couldn't help but laugh. "That's it . . . for today. That's the 'Beginning' framework. Everything stems from S.C.A.L.E."

"This is awesome. What's next?"

"That is a good question," she said. "I am heading overseas this afternoon and will be back late next week. There are two frameworks you need to learn in order to be able to impact your team's results this quarter. The sooner the better. What do you propose to do while I'm gone?" She returned to her desk, crossed a leg, and leaned back in her chair.

Arlo noticed her glance at the clock on her desk. He knew that she was a busy executive and would probably have zero interest in or availability for phone calls while overseas. But he needed help fast, and she knew that. It also felt like she was expecting him to show a commitment to the process.

"You mentioned that you've shared these frameworks with your managers and with Sales Enablement. Is there someone who would be willing to meet with me in your absence?" He pursed his lips and raised an eyebrow, doing his best to indicate that he knew it was an ambitious ask.

Alex surveyed his face but sat expressionless for what seemed like an eternity. "I'll tell you what. It would not be fair for me to ask one person to spend the amount of time it will take with you next week." His shoulders sank but he maintained eye contact. "However, I can spread it out over a few managers—if you don't mind bouncing around a little."

Arlo barely let her finish. "Not at all! Bounce me around. I'll take what I can get."

"You'll have to come over here early all next week."

"Done!" He was ecstatic.

"Sponge, not stone?" she said.

"Total sponge!"

She looked at his notebook. "You must bring that every day."

"Every day!" he repeated. He gathered his things. He'd learned once that once you close the deal—stop selling.

"Arlo, let me ask you. What happens if you miss an appointment with a member of my team? Because a meeting came up, the elevator got stuck, a horde of locusts swarms the city?" She crossed to the door, which meant the meeting was concluding.

"It means you will never speak to me again."

She smiled. "Oh, I'll speak to you again, Arlo. I'm not emotionally invested in your commitment. But I bet it won't be at the coffee shop. As I understand it, if you don't make an impact—and fast—you'll no longer be working next door. Is that correct?"

His attempt at levity had been crushed. "Yeah. That's correct." No matter how he tried to push it out of his mind, she kept coming back to it. He rose to leave and shook her hand.

"You have my commitment to provide you access to the people who will give you the tools you need to not just keep your job, but truly make the impact you want to make. I expect you to ask questions, observe, and document three lessons learned from each conversation. Let's meet when I return. What will you share with me then?"

"How about my notebook and how I plan to apply what I learn?" he said.

"Let's be specific. Why don't you summarize each meeting into three high-level bullet points? You can share those with me. Does that sound fair?" Arlo nodded in agreement.

"And, Arlo," she said in a serious tone, "do not roll this out with your team until we meet next week, okay?"

"You got it!" He scurried down the hall toward the elevator.

■ ■ ■

Arlo spent Saturday and Sunday reflecting on what he had learned about S.C.A.L.E. and anxiously anticipating what was to come the following week. He had a nervous feeling in the pit of his stomach, which he knew was part anticipation, part dread. He was excited about the journey he was about to undertake, but worried that maybe Alex had more faith in him than was due. Perhaps he wasn't cut out to be a great coach. If S.C.A.L.E. was just the beginning, he felt pretty far behind from the start.

He got e-mail invitations from five of Alex's managers with appointments each morning. And one from Alex's assistant for lunch on Friday afternoon.

Notes

[1] The S.C.A.L.E. framework was adapted from the SCARF model to apply to sales. David Rock. "SCARF: A Brain-Based Model for Collaborating with and Influencing Others." NeuroLeadership Journal no. 1 (2008), https://www.epa.gov/sites/production/files/2015-09/documents/thurs_georgia_9_10_915_covello.pdf

8

THE FIRST SECRET:
C IS FOR CHALLENGE

The MAStery framework helps us to decide how to coach the challenge we decide to address.

This time the elevator opened to a low buzz on the forty-fifth floor. It was that buzz of the day starting with people chatting in their pre-caffeinated morning voices.

The meeting request he'd received from Charles on Friday afternoon was for Monday 7 a.m. Arlo had loitered in the coffee shop (much to the barista's chagrin) for thirty minutes in order not to be late, and made it up to the forty-fifth floor exactly three minutes early. He typed his name into the visitor's pad at the empty reception desk. *Your host has been notified.*

When Charles appeared a few minutes later, he was considerably younger than Arlo had anticipated. His ConnectIn profile had said that Charles was a mid-market sales manager and had been at

GigaTech for three years. He began as an account manager after working as an inside sales rep for a few years at another company and was promoted to this role the previous year. Charles peeked his head from around the corner and silently gestured for Arlo to follow.

Even at this hour, Charles had the disheveled look of someone who had been working for hours. His checkered oxford sleeves were rolled up to the elbow. Brown hair just long enough that he probably missed a haircut last week. There were signs of dry erase marker residue on his forefinger, likely from a hasty erase mid-sentence. He carried a well-worn leather moleskin journal, which he probably took to meetings all day.

"Hi Arlo. Nice to meet you." His tone was neither enthusiastic nor labored. Just detached.

Arlo followed Charles around a series of corridors and open work-spaces with most seats already occupied by sales reps on phones. Very different from the culture at his company. "This team covers Europe and the east coast. While the rest of the city is just getting out of bed, these folks are setting up appointments or closing deals." He was not bragging . . . just stating facts.

Charles stopped at a glass conference room door etched with the number "33" from floor to ceiling. Most companies he knew of used inventors, mathematicians, landmarks, *Star Wars* characters, cities, and such to name their conference rooms. Just numbers. *It must be some kind of efficiency thing Alex came up with.*

As they sat, Charles began. Again with the facts. "So you've met Alex."

"Yes, she's great. I'm really thankful for your time," Arlo said, hoping to lighten the mood a bit. Charles smiled genuinely but wasn't biting.

"Well, we've got an hour to cover a lot of ground. Shall we?" He wrote "Challenge" on the whiteboard. "The first of the five secrets for coaching salespeople is to identify the challenge. In other words, what are we trying to impact?"

Arlo got his notebook out and swiveled one of the conference room chairs toward Charles, dropping his backpack to the floor.

"That doesn't sound so secret," Arlo said matter-of-factly. "Isn't that usually fairly obvious? Sales is ultimately about revenue. Either we close or we don't." After a weekend of studying the notes from his meeting with Alex, Arlo was determined to give more thoughtful responses than he had on Friday.

Charles sighed lightly—a patient disapproval. "You would think so. If it was as simple as just directing salespeople to make calls, have meetings, and close deals, I think many more people would be successful sales managers. And you probably wouldn't be meeting with me this morning."

Arlo thought that may have trivialized his point, but he was willing to hear Charles out. *Sponge, not a rock.*

"Most managers either fail to coach at all, feeling that rigor around activity will win the numbers game that they believe sales to be.

Or, worse." Charles leaned over the conference table in a conspiratorial tone. "I was a pretty good sales person before I became a manager. Not top of the leaderboard all the time, but I was consistent. I did the activity, I followed the methodology, I knew my numbers, and I hit them."

Arlo could relate.

"My manager at my old company would pull me into his office for the most ridiculous conversations about things that had no impact on my sales efficiency or results. It was maddening. I remember one time he wanted to talk to me about writing *discovery letters* to my prospects after every discovery call and how he wanted me to spend at least fifteen minutes on each one. I was selling a pretty transactional product to the same stakeholder all day every day. I uncovered pain, identified stakeholders, found out how they were going to pay, and we agreed to a next step . . . *that I documented in the CRM* . . . but this guy wanted me to spend a couple of hours a day writing a long narrative that no one would ever read. It was a giant waste of time. It had nothing to do with the goals of the company," he said. "I call that nit-picking. Not coaching. How do managers coach salespeople on things that don't move the needle?"

In fact, Arlo'd had many conversations that had little impact on measurable goals. His recent meetings with Seth, Samantha, and Derek had all focused on nit-picky items that annoyed Arlo, but even if fixed, they had no chance of helping them achieve quota. "I'd imagine quite a few," he said.

"What impact do you think that has on S.C.A.L.E. drivers?" Charles said.

"Well, that's not going to create a relationship conducive to coaching. So then how do you choose what to focus on?"

"Identifying the Challenge requires me to determine what the lowest hanging opportunity is with the highest reward for my salesperson," Charles said. "Where is the gap between where a sales rep is today, and where I need them to be in order to effectively and consistently impact the metrics that move the business? For me, it's revenue, deal size, velocity, and vertical markets."

"You do this for every coaching conversation?" Arlo asked.

"I sure do. It also forces us, as a management team, to align on high-level goals so that in coaching conversations we are coaching MAStery," he wrote the word on the board, "toward what matters."

"MAStery?" Arlo asked, taking notes. Charles was ahead of him and drawing three pillars on the whiteboard.

"You learned the S.C.A.L.E. framework yesterday, which is how we create and maintain an environment conducive to a coaching relationship with our reps. Today you get your second framework. It's called the MAStery framework."

Arlo liked the sound of that. He felt that he had squeezed the very last drop out of tips and tricks. MAStery was music to his ears!

"This is one of the very first images that Alex shows her managers," Charles said. "The MAStery framework consists of three pillars."

In each pillar, he had written a word—Mindset, Activity, and Skillset.

"Success in anything we attempt to do is a direct function of these three things."

Arlo turned to a fresh page and drew the image, remembering that he had promised Alex notes from each meeting.

"The MAStery framework helps us to decide how to coach the challenge we decide to address," Charles said.

"How to coach?" Arlo asked.

"Yes. There are a million things we could choose to coach, and as many variables as to how we can go about it. I don't have time for that. I am ultimately trying to achieve a goal, together with my sales reps, so my job is to look for the lowest hanging fruit with the greatest opportunity for increased effectiveness. Once I have identified that, I need to know what kind of challenge my sales rep is facing."

Arlo was lost. That pit in his stomach was back.

"Don't worry. It's easier than it sounds," Charles said. "The 'M' in MAStery stands for Mindset. There are only two types of Mindset. Supportive mindsets are those which reinforce our ability to accomplish things and be successful. For instance, a supportive mindset for a salesperson would be: *It is okay to quickly disqualify prospects who do not have a problem I can solve.* Because it is obviously a waste of time for a salesperson to try to convince someone to buy something that they don't need, right?"

"Exactly," Arlo said, relieved that this framework wasn't sounding terribly complex. "Or, *talking about money demonstrates business acumen and maturity,*" he offered.

"That's a great one! I'm going to remember that," Charles said. "So, then, on the other side of that coin are unsupportive mindsets. Unfortunately, these are plentiful on the sales floor. These reinforce our inability to execute, grow, and be successful. For instance, an unsupportive mindset for a salesperson would be: *During demos I need to educate the prospect and show everything the product can do, otherwise my prospect won't buy.*"

"That sounds like a self-fulfilling prophecy!"

"If I ever heard one . . ." Charles smiled and actually laughed.

"How about, *I need to thoroughly educate my prospect before they buy from me?* That drives me crazy," said Arlo, feeling confident.

"Yes! That is an absolutely unsupportive mindset. The thing is that salespeople often have difficulty understanding that the mindset is not fact. Just an individual perspective. Our Challenge then becomes to help them move from that perspective to one that is more supportive by leveraging the other two pillars of MAStery," Charles said.

"Umm . . . Okay. How the heck do you do that?" he said, losing enthusiasm.

Charles laughed. "Like I said, it's not as hard as you would think. But first, let's look at Activity," he said. "Activity is really just the things a salesperson does every day. Cold calling. E-mailing. Discovery. Presentations and demos. Proposals. In-person meetings. Trade shows. Social media. Networking. I could go on."

"That makes sense. If you're not doing anything, you're not going to get anywhere."

"Precisely. Or if you are doing the wrong thing. . . ." Charles added. "I had one sales rep who spent a whole week sourcing and calling prospects who just happened to be our customers. Totally my fault. All of his search criteria was right, I just hadn't given him a black list." Charles buried his head in his hands.

"Ouch!" Arlo said, noting the use of a story to develop rapport. *This guy is good.* "So we're talking about rigor and the right activity then?"

"That's correct. The final pillar of MAStery is Skillset. Pretty self-explanatory. Skillset is just the ability to do something well or a level of expertise," said Charles.

"You can't coach someone on something they haven't been trained to do," Arlo remembered. "So, obviously, if someone is unable to do something well, they cannot achieve MAStery. That makes total sense. Then how do you use this in tandem with the challenge you have identified?"

"It just so happens that I have a coaching conversation scheduled this morning with an AE who is struggling. So let me show you how I do it." Charles sat down right next to Arlo, flipping to notes he'd made in his journal.

"At our Sales Kick Off last month, Alex underscored that *discovery* is our primary focus this quarter. We need to disqualify early, uncover pain we can solve, quantify that pain, and create urgency to increase velocity in the pipeline. As a management team, we determined that discovery is the overarching means to this end." He pointed to his notes on the subject and paused to ensure that Arlo was following.

Arlo nodded. He was impressed that Alex's organization was able to come together around a core concept. It seemed that the more his team tried to simplify, the more complex the objectives seemed to become. He was hopeful that he'd be able to take away some easy ways that his management team could come together as well.

"With that in mind, this account executive has been struggling with deals that seem to get stuck in her pipeline after she does a demo. I've reviewed a few of her recorded demos and it's clear that she's got two Challenges. One, she is not doing a deep dive into uncovering pain, and two, she is not creating urgency as a result," he said.

"Okay, so both of those issues fall under the primary focus from Alex." Arlo took the cue. "But it seems to me that if you can get her uncovering pain more effectively, then urgency will follow. That would make it the lowest hanging opportunity with the highest value. So it sounds like you should focus your energy there."

"Well done! I agree. See, that wasn't so hard, was it? So the Challenge is uncovering pain during discovery. What we haven't agreed upon is where it fits on the MAStery framework," he said.

"Well, I think that depends," Arlo said. "If she doesn't think that uncovering pain is important, or maybe doesn't think that it's any of her business, then it would be a Mindset issue. If she's just not following up ineffectively and doesn't have agreed upon next steps in the CRM, then it's Activity." He paused, a little stuck. "I'm not sure how to determine if it is a Skillset issue."

"That one's easy as well. I know that she has been trained on our sales frameworks, which include a method for uncovering pain. She's actually been certified in it pretty recently. So she has demonstrated the Skillset," Charles said.

"Let's take a look at the CRM, then," Arlo said. They huddled around Charles' laptop and found that Sam had consistent entries with dates of follow-up conversations, which aligned with sales stages and calendar invites accepted by prospects. "Looks like we've got a Mindset issue!" Charles agreed. He surveyed Arlo, who was drawing and writing frantically in his journal.

"So, I've identified a Challenge that directly relates to the goals of the organization, and I understand the type of Challenge I am dealing with. Now I can do the rest of my pre-work to ensure that we have a productive conversation." Charles closed his laptop and stood up to erase the board.

"Questions?" Charles said, rolling up a sleeve that had slipped to his wrist.

"So? What's the rest of the pre-work?"

"That, my friend, is for tomorrow," Charles said. "I think you're meeting with Olivia, right?" Arlo checked his phone.

"Yeah, Olivia at 7 a.m.," he said. "You guys are an early-rising team!"

"Yeah, some of us actually manage reps who work the east coast and Europe, while others like to get this kind of planning work done first thing so that we keep our eye on the right things throughout the day."

Arlo was a little surprised that the first secret hadn't been too daunting. His mind was racing at the work he needed to do to be able to implement it. "So when it comes to aligning the challenge with the goals of the business, how do you arrive at those goals?"

"Luckily for us, we work with Alex. She does a great job of focusing the team. In my experience, in spite of all of the acronyms used to create efficiency, and all of the vanity metrics and reports you can spit out of a CRM . . . there are only a few high-level things that need your constant attention. If the focus is maintained, the results will follow. Too many dashboards and tools are really just a distraction. Alex always encourages us to simplify. Prove it out in analog before we go automating things digitally. She says, *'Everyone on the sales floor should be able to articulate and understand the goals of the department in a single sentence.'* That isn't to say that it's easy. But that's the work of managers and leadership. Then you can pilot the organization," he said.

"Does it matter what method you use to get there?" said Arlo.

"Not at all. Alex has trained people on the C.O.A.C.H. framework who use KPI to align; some like MBO, others like OKR, still others prefer E-I-E-I-O," he laughed.

It took him a minute to understand, then Arlo laughed too. "Yeah there are a ton of acronyms. The universal concept basically seems to be—focus and tracking and accountability."

"Ultimately, yes. Don't knock acronyms in front of Alex though! Two things she's a huge fan of—acronyms, and the Michael Jordan era Chicago Bulls!" Charles raised his eyebrows and clenched his teeth—as though he'd said too much. "Arlo, it was nice meeting and good luck to you." They shook hands.

Arlo was impressed with Charles. He felt that even though they were about the same age, Charles was probably light years ahead in management development. It was a good target for Arlo to shoot for, and a clear indication that there were solutions to all of the problems he was encountering. He wondered if Alex put them together first for a reason. It seemed like something she would do.

When he returned to his office, Arlo passed the desks of his sales reps imagining giant word bubbles floating over their heads— "Mindset," "Activity," "Skillset." They no longer looked so enigmatic.

At his desk, Arlo wrote down his three lessons learned from The First Secret: *Challenge.*

CHALLENGE

- ENSURE ALIGNMENT OF ENTIRE DEPARTMENT ON THE OBJECTIVES THAT WILL MEASURABLY MOVE THE METRICS IMPORTANT TO SUCCESS THEN FOCUS ONLY ON THOSE CHALLENGES

- IDENTIFY THE CHALLENGE WHICH PRESENTS THE LOWEST HANGING OPPORTUNITY WITH THE HIGHEST POTENTIAL REWARD. ONLY ONE CHALLENGE CAN BE COACHED AT ONE TIME.

- USE THE MASTERY FRAMEWORK TO DETERMINE WHAT TYPE OF CHALLENGE THE INDIVIDUAL IS DEALING WITH: MINDSET, ACTIVITY, OR SKILLSET

9

UNDERSTANDING HIS TEAM

Arlo had spent the night reviewing the Sales Kick-Off deck from this quarter to try to find something actionable among all of the slides—total revenue, individual awards, new product features, and new hires. There was nothing there. Just a ton of fuzzy language around commitment and leaning in, market shifts, and some marketing buzzwords about product positioning. No clear focus. The thesis was "Sell More Stuff." But a clear plan was nonexistent. And that wasn't gonna cut it.

What Charles had taught him yesterday was simple. In theory. But the goals for the company and for his team were not completely clear. Without clearly understanding where they were trying to go, Arlo knew it would be difficult to identify the right challenges his people were experiencing.

So, with an Uno's pie box fresh out of the oven, he plopped down on the couch his mother gave him. Using sticky notes, he began to pick apart the critical elements from the Sales Kick Off presentation deck. Each dashboard, each report, the goals that were presented to the board of directors, and the highlights communicated from the management team.

By two in the morning, through an unsophisticated process of elimination, he felt confident that the primary objective for his team this quarter was to *grow revenue from selling larger deals.*

The sales team had thrived on closing whatever was fast and easy, and while that was fantastic, they were leaving a ton of money on the table, and the customer acquisition costs were skyrocketing.

New competitors had entered the field, old competitors had new products, and his company was no longer particularly disruptive. Their answer to the competitive landscape was to add products that salespeople could offer, but the team continued selling what they were comfortable with, for the most part. Arlo's team was struggling in the transition from working simple transactional deals to having to conduct discovery with different stakeholders to find the right solution. Big deals were expected of his team even though they worked with small and medium-sized businesses (SMB).

He had lost a few reps early on because the new direction was not one they had signed up for. He understood now that S.C.A.L.E. was at work. Their Certainty drivers and Equity drivers had been negatively impacted by what some felt was a sudden change.

Status paralyzed others, who were accustomed to exceeding quota effortlessly and found themselves struggling now.

He thought about the MAStery pillars impacting his team. Samantha just wasn't getting the Activity done. Her numbers were way off, and her focus on yoga was having a big impact on her success. Derek had some skillset issues, which Arlo now realized required some more formal training to best use his energy. Jackie, as good as she was, really had a "me against the world" mindset, which was not going to serve her well much longer. Her inability to work as part of a team presented a challenge to collaboration and team cohesiveness.

Lindsay was a puzzle. Arlo felt at first that she had a skill gap too, but that couldn't be the case. She was able to hit her number consistently—but she just stopped at that point and never ever wanted to take that next step. He reasoned that it was actually a Mindset challenge with her.

And Seth. Well, depending upon the challenge, Seth was a mixed bag. He seemed to have a very supportive mindset around the team and the work. He had been trained on how to do the job. Arlo reasoned that Seth just needed some accountability regarding Activity.

It felt like progress—having this new lens to see the team through. It cut through any emotion or any opinion and allowed Arlo to see each individual in relation to the goals of the team.

Around 3 a.m., he fell asleep where he sat.

10

THE SECOND SECRET: O IS FOR OUTLINE

*You cannot coach someone if you don't understand
where they need to go.*

There was no time for coffee the next morning. Arlo dashed out of the elevator on the forty-fifth floor and raced to the visitor's pad in the empty lobby to key in his name just as the clock showed 7 a.m. *Phew!* He knew that late would not have sat well with Alex.

Olivia almost literally bounced around the corner. She was one of GigaTech's mid-market sales managers. Judging by the dashboards on the sales floor, her team was killing it this quarter.

She had a spring in her step and a big smile on her face. Not the bouncing a teenager does as they bound into a room; this was the enthusiasm of someone who probably had inexhaustible energy.

Arlo thought it was much more than any human should have this early in the morning, but he was glad because he needed it.

Extending her hand as she approached, it was clear that she was accustomed to crossing a room faster than anyone she came to greet. Like parkour without any obstacles.

She looked a bit like she might have once felt at home in a session on a half-pipe with her skateboard, dropping in to hoots and hollers from bystanders feeding off of her raw enthusiasm and fearlessness.

"I'm Olivia! So nice to meet you!" she said, smiling and cocking her head to one side like how a teacher might greet a new transfer student. She was in her thirties, and while he hadn't had time to look up her profile on ConnectIn, he'd wager that she had been a successful sales person.

Conversation came easy to her. Her eye contact was natural and engaging, and she directed the conversation through questions that clearly uncovered information she wanted without being off-putting or awkward.

"Alex sent me a quick note to meet with you about C.O.A.C.H. Other than that, I don't have a ton of context," she smiled. "How did you two connect?"

"We actually met in the cafe downstairs. I tried to steal her coffee," he said, following her through the low buzz of the sales floor. Some familiar faces smiled.

"You tried to steal her coffee? Like on the street?" She stopped for a second, definitely not expecting this response.

"At the cafe. I wasn't paying attention. I had a management team meeting that morning and was dreading it. I was totally in my head, trying to come up with my spin on what I was going to do to fix things . . ." he said.

"Ha! I remember those days." They picked up walking again. "Coming in every month with an elaborate explanation for why I had a variance to my target. Whether I was trending ahead or behind, I had to have a rationale," she said. "And frankly, I usually had no idea!"

She stopped in the kitchen. "Coffee?" she offered, grabbing yogurt and a piece of fruit from the fridge.

"Yes, please!" She was a life saver. He grabbed a mug from the shelf above the sink and surveyed the buttons on the coffee machine.

"Cappuccino, espresso, latte, Americano?" she listed them off.

"How about a cortado?" he said, laughing to himself and rocking back on his heels at his inside joke.

"Um . . . yeah, it doesn't do that. Whatever that is," she shrugged.

"Plain old coffee would be fine," he said. "You said you remember those days. So I take it that that's not the way you do things anymore?"

"Charles probably explained how the management team aligns around a common focus? Well, that becomes the bottom line. Of course, we're still accountable to the numbers, but the substance of our meetings is about how we are managing and coaching to the common focus. We don't waste energy in meetings discussing things we can glean from data and reports," Olivia said, offering him the cream and sugar.

"No thanks," he said. "So what do you talk about in your management team meetings?"

"We talk about how we are developing our people. The Challenges we've identified, and how we are addressing them." She led him to a conference room with a giant "7" etched on the glass door. "Come on in."

"So, as a management team you have conversations about professional development?" he asked.

"As it relates to the goals of the business, yes." She sucked her teeth, noticing his confusion. "Looks like that concept is new to you."

"Completely!"

"I've found it to be much more productive, and I get the support and collaboration of my peers. They have insight into the Challenges I'm facing, and we all have different backgrounds and skills, so our approaches differ and I learn a lot. It also keeps us honest. In other companies, I have felt as though management team meetings were a series of one-upmanship, or a game of gotcha! We don't play games here. We work together." She folded her hands.

"That's really impressive. Sounds idyllic." He thought about the culture at VizuData. Peer collaboration typically only took place at company all-hands meetings when they were called upon to build a pasta castle, or trebuchet that could fling a ping pong ball the longest distance into a cup.

But there was no collaboration around the work itself. Management team meetings like the one Arlo'd had the prior week were anything but supportive.

"I don't know about idyllic. It's productive though. We work hard. We're not over here dancing through the daisies and singing 'Kumbaya.' We're acutely focused on what matters. That's typically challenging enough for a sales team, so there's no need to invite the unnecessary."

"Agreed." He liked that sentiment, and got out his journal.

"Are you ready for the second secret of coaching salespeople, Arlo?" she said.

He finished writing and looked up. "I most certainly am."

"Write down 'Outline the Path to Success' in your notebook," she said. "It sounds obvious, right?" she continued. "You cannot coach someone if you don't understand where they need to go. But we've got to go one step further than where they need to go. We need to know how they are going to get there."

"So not just the gap between the Challenge and the goal. But the path?"

"Correct. Good coaches take you along a path. They don't just stand at one end and point in a direction, slap you on the back, and say 'go for it.'" She was one of those people who laughed on the inhale instead of the exhale, kind of seal-like. It made whatever she was laughing at even funnier.

"I've had those coaches before." He thought of Gabe who had just told him that he was 'here for you . . . whatever you need . . .'"

Go for it!

"So it's our job to spell it out step by step then?" he asked.

"No. Not step by step. That's exhausting, and it's not coaching. That would be training," she said. "Our job is to know at least one reasonable path to success before having a coaching conversation so that we can guide the sales rep while still rewarding their Autonomy driver from S.C.A.L.E." Olivia looked for recognition in Arlo's eyes.

Arlo loved that he knew exactly what this meant. All of this new language was beginning to fit together. He grabbed the ball.

"So you're saying that you don't have to spell it out, but as a coach you have to understand your system well enough to direct the salesperson within to reach a desired outcome," he said.

"Nailed it!" She reached over to give him a high-five. "Here's an example. I'm going to have a conversation today with one of my reps named Kai. He's consistent, though he gets a little lazy and goes rogue sometimes. Do you remember what GigaTech's focus is this quarter?"

"Discovery. Uncovering pain that you can fix," Arlo said.

"Right. Well, Kai's challenge is that he's not getting permission to ask prospects questions. Since he's not getting permission, he gets five minutes into discovery, and the prospects are annoyed and feel like they're being interrogated. He senses that and then he bails out and starts doing his feature and benefit dance. Do you know where that leads?"

He knew. "Nowhere."

"Absolutely, nowhere. It leads to a request for more information. Then he ends up checking in, following up, touching base, and circling back forever!" That laugh again. It made Arlo laugh too. "So I gotta get him back on track. It's the lowest hanging opportunity for him with the biggest reward. If he just gets permission to ask questions, he'll get to pain if it exists, or he'll be able to disqualify quickly and move on."

"OK so now you Outline the path to success?" he asked.

She looked at him like he should know better. "First, we have to know . . ."

"What pillar of MAStery we're dealing with!" He saved himself.

"Right! We can scratch off the skills pillar because he has done it before successfully for months. I am pretty certain that he understands the importance as well. My hunch is that he's just fallen out of practice. So it's an Activity thing."

"Okay. So how do you get him doing it?" Arlo asked.

"The Outline for an Activity Challenge is one of the easier ones. He needs to come up with his own way to simply remember to do what he has been trained to do. I'm going to validate that he is still competent at getting permission to ask questions, ensure that he still believes it is beneficial to the sales process by showing him the results he's getting by not asking questions, then I'm going to ask him to come up with a plan for how he will remember to do it for the next week," she said. "That's my Outline."

"It sounds like you're using Autonomy by letting him choose how he is going to remember, and by asking him what he should do . . . well that's Equity," he said.

"Very good! Did you hear what I am doing with Mindset and Skill?"

"Huh?"

"Well. If we have identified that every Challenge is rooted in the weakness of a specific pillar, then we can leverage the strong pillars as part of our outline. So since the weakness exists in this rep's Activity regarding asking permission to ask questions, I am going to use the fact that he knows how, which is Skillset, and that he believes it's important, which is Mindset, in order to get him on the right path."

"That is brilliant!" He slapped the conference room table with his palm.

"I don't know about brilliant. But it is effective!" Oh, that laugh was insane. It had to drive the sales floor crazy. Now it was more like a goose choking. "If I determined that it was a Mindset challenge . . ."

"You would leverage Skillset and create an Activity that would evolve the Mindset to a supportive one based upon outcomes," he blurted out. It was very logical. "And if it was a Skillset challenge you would . . ." He thought for a minute.

"Ahh . . ." he wagged his index finger as if Olivia had been trying to trick him. "If it was a Skillset Challenge, then you have a training opportunity."

"Voila," she said with a high-five across the table.

"Voila, indeed." He folded his arms across his chest, nodding slowly. "That is very good."

"The best part is that I have gotten to the point where I do this all in my head now. Alex says, 'It's irresponsible to enter into a coaching conversation with a sales rep without any idea of where you are intending it to go. Or hoping you'll find out along the way.' That's not coaching. That's called chatting."

She had a point. There were times Arlo had gone into coaching conversations without preparation other than to identify that there was a problem. The conversation would then meander or follow an awkward track of Arlo dragging the salesperson to a conclusion. The salesperson would admit to the problem and offer a vapid pledge to "do better" in the hope of ending the conversation. An offer Arlo had often accepted because he, too, felt uncomfortable. He now realized the reason why so few managers had coaching conversations—they could be unproductive and awkward.

"So, you don't go into any coaching conversations without a mental Outline of the path to success?"

"No way. It's reckless. I risk losing credibility with my sales rep or worse, having a conversation that is primarily punitive and offers no solutions. I've been there before. It breeds resentment and completely undercuts productivity."

Arlo understood completely. "I appreciate you spending time with me this morning, Olivia."

"You bet. Good luck, Arlo. I think you're on the right . . . path." She laughed that laugh and led him out.

■ ■ ■

Back at his desk, Arlo leaned back in his chair, staring at the ceiling. How had these concepts eluded him for so long? This was not rocket science. *Just people science,* he guessed.

He took out his journal to write three bullets for The Second Secret: *Outlining the Path to Success*:

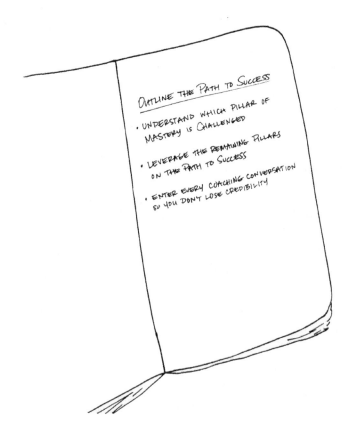

OUTLINE THE PATH TO SUCCESS

· UNDERSTAND WHICH PILLAR OF MASTERY IS CHALLENGED

· LEVERAGE THE REMAINING PILLARS ON THE PATH TO SUCCESS

· ENTER EVERY COACHING CONVERSATION SO YOU DON'T LOSE CREDIBILITY

11

THE THIRD SECRET: A IS FOR ACTION PLAN

If, every time you met with your manager for a coaching session, they asked you what Action you were going to take to overcome a specific Challenge, or achieve a goal, pretty soon you'd come prepared for that conversation.

After a blur of a day and his first good night's sleep in nearly a week, Arlo found himself back on the forty-fifth floor on Wednesday, eager to unlock the rest of the secrets.

Conference room 25 was a little smaller and further out than the others at GigaTech, which was probably a good thing because Amir was animated as he crossed from corner to corner. He was an SMB sales manager, like Arlo.

He was passionately explaining to Arlo—in a voice that was a tad squeaky for someone his late twenties—everything he had just learned in a leadership conference two days prior. Amir was fascinating to watch. His every statement was a full-body experience. It was as if his thoughts emanated from his pacing around the tiny room, gathered in his diaphragm where they were infused with helium, rose through his chest where he hand-pantomimed them to his audience, and finally came out of his mouth with the lilt of a prepubescent boy.

It was a fascinating spectacle. With a bag of popcorn, Arlo could have watched this show all day.

"It was awesome!" Amir said. "There were all of these exercises to help newer managers like me to be able to understand ourselves better," he said. "I know it sounds crazy, but Alex always says that you cannot manage effectively unless you understand yourself. That it all starts with you."

Arlo sat back as Amir organized two three-ring binders and a full legal pad of notes across the small conference table. Amir was a small guy with bird-like movements. His dry-fit golf shirt was neatly tucked into his jeans. This guy definitely uses a standing desk, Arlo thought . . . with a treadmill!

"Wow! That's a ton of information. It sounds like you came back with a lot of good ideas."

"I did. That's the problem," Amir said.

Arlo furrowed his brow. "I don't understand."

"I've got so much information in my head that if I don't come up with a plan, it will all be wasted—and the only benefit I'll have received is two days of enlightenment which ended up having no impact," he said. "That's not going to wash with Alex."

Arlo thought of the many times either he or one of his colleagues had attended conferences and returned with a head full of ideas only to be stymied by the demands of their existing workload. He could totally relate. But the clock was ticking on this one-hour meeting and he was anxious to get Amir to share the third secret.

"Good luck with all that" he said a bit sheepishly, borrowing from the technique he used to get off the phone with nosy relatives. "I don't want to take too much time away from your work on that plan. Was there anything you wanted to share with me today?" He worried that he may be sounding a little pushy, but damn it, his job depended on this.

Amir stopped moving for the first time. He looked at Arlo and sat down. "Dude . . . this is it!" His arms swept across the table.

Arlo was confused. "What is what?" he managed.

"This!" Amir swept his arms again, as if the obvious was invisible. "This is the Third Secret!" His head nodded, seeking recognition. There was none forthcoming.

"You want me to study this Leadership Conference stuff?" Arlo asked. When he didn't understand something he had a tendency to get agitated.

"No, Arlo." Amir was speaking slowly now, in his high-pitched voice, as if to a small child. "I want you . . . to help me to develop . . ." he popped open a marker and jumped up to the board, "an Action Plan. The third secret is Action Plan." He turned to Arlo with eyebrows raised in invitation.

"Action Plan," Arlo repeated.

"That's correct. See, when Alex comes back on Friday, she is going to ask me how the conference was. I made the mistake, when I first started working here, of attending a trade show to learn more about the competition and when she asked me how it was, I told her it was great!"

Arlo nodded. "And?"

"Right! Any normal human being would think that was a satisfactory answer. But you've met Alex." He gestured toward Arlo, looking for agreement. "Well, I thought that would be a satisfactory answer. Let's just say it wasn't." He sat down and leaned toward Arlo as if to tell him something in confidence.

"She began by uncovering the Challenges I was having at the time in understanding our winning zone versus the competition. She had already Outlined the path I would need to take to help my team to use pain questions in competitive deals, but then we worked together to come up with a detailed Action plan for how I was going to integrate competitive insights from the tradeshow into our messaging," he said.

"So Alex worked with you to develop the Action Plan?" Arlo asked.

"She sure did. I'll show you how." Amir rose to return to the whiteboard.

"But if she works with you on these things, then why are we doing it now? Before your meeting with her?"

"If, every time you met with your manager for a coaching session, they asked you what Action you were going to take to overcome a specific Challenge, or achieve a goal, pretty soon you'd come prepared for that conversation, right?" He shrugged.

Arlo thought about it and began to understand what Amir meant. "So it's like a conditioned response. Because she consistently approaches your coaching conversations in the same manner, you've come to know what to expect?"

"Absolutely. Don't forget that we have all been trained to coach the same way. So, the culture of the organization has shifted. We all know what to expect. We all know why. So now, Alex offers guidance based upon her experience and knowledge, but her managers do a lot of self-coaching and peer-coaching. Like what we're doing today."

"That must free up a lot of time!"

"It frees up time, it keeps us all aligned, and when we coach ourselves, we actually become better coaches of our team," Amir said. "Now with newer, or more junior team members, we can't always expect that they have developed the skills to create a viable Action Plan. In those cases, our role is to guide the Action Plan like Alex did with me."

"How do you do that?" asked Arlo.

"It's really easier than it sounds. You ultimately want to ensure that Actions are MET." Amir wrote this on the board. "Measurable, Empowered, and Time-Sensitive. That's it."

"Well, that's easier than OKRs, SMART goals, KPIs, and the rest," Arlo said.

"Nothing wrong with those. Choose your acronym!" Amir flailed his hands in the air. "But it's a given that managers are busy. Coaching falls to the wayside when it is too rigorous or complicated, or the follow-up is too time-consuming. You don't want Action to be a science project; you just want goals to be . . ."

"MET!" Arlo chimed in. "I get it."

"Yes! The biggest challenge for the coach is to ensure that we are helping to break what could be a very large goal into easily

MET increments. As with anything, practice makes it easier. So let's define it," he said.

"Measurable means just that. There should be an easy, transparent way of quantifying the Action. Ideally this is something that takes place inside of a technology tool like a CRM, calendar, or other real-time way. But that's not always the case. Regardless, we need to be able to tell that effort has been made.

"Empowered means that the individual being coached must be in a position to successfully complete the Action. This can mean anything from decision-making authority to access to tools and training, resources, or just ensuring that you are only holding people accountable for things within their control," Amir said. Arlo began taking notes.

"Closed business would NOT be a good Action Plan. Salespeople cannot control their prospects' decision to purchase. Making a certain number of cold calls, however, is completely within a sales person's control. The role of the manager is to know how many of those calls a salesperson needs to make—based upon previous experience or some hypothesis to hit their closed business goal."

"So we should manage the outcomes through the Action. The means to the end . . . not the end, then?" Arlo said.

"You got it. Finally, you want to ensure that you are following up and evaluating success by making these Actions Time-Sensitive.

This makes each coaching conversation nice and finite, keeping the focus on what matters."

"So are you saying that each member of the team, at any given time, is working toward a MET goal that you've both agreed upon?" Arlo was fascinated.

"Absolutely. Otherwise it's chaos and plate spinning!" Amir leapt from corner to corner, simulating a circus plate-spinner.

Arlo was now serious, thinking about his mode of functioning. His team, viewed in this light, was operating chaotically. He had no specific timelines in place for the loose commitments they had made. Many of the goals he had set, were things like "do a better job of this" or "work on ratcheting up the volume of that." In hindsight, there was a clear reason why his team's goals were actually unMET. In many of these conversations, his reps were willing to commit to anything as long as they could just get out of the room. Who could blame them?

"Watching the action plan come to life is like self-working magic. Having done the work of identifying the Challenge and Outlining the opportunity, I have a clear idea of where the coaching conversation is going, which allows me to facilitate the salesperson's journey by asking a bunch of questions, just as we do in discovery with prospects. In the end, one of three outcomes occurs:

My Plan: The same plan that I had conceived, but since we've worked together to create it, the salesperson has ownership and buy in.

A Better Plan: Often, the salesperson will have additional insights and come up with a slightly or significantly better idea than what I had in mind.

A Plan that Won't Work: Occasionally, the salesperson will get off track and come to a conclusion that's not realistic or that won't have the desired impact. But having done the pre-work, I will know this and can work with the rep to calibrate a MET goal that is primed for success."

Amir paused, as Arlo made notes in his notebook. When Arlo looked up, he continued.

"Don't let reps set actions that are unreasonable. Sometimes, salespeople will say whatever they think they need to in order to get out of the room. Often, coaching conversations remind them of interactions with parents scolding them about behavior, or a teacher, or some other authority figure," he said.

"They might commit to doing something exactly the right way every time the opportunity presents itself. Chances are, even your best salespeople can't be held to that bar, so it's unrealistic to have a salesperson in need of coaching make this type of commitment. It will only lead to frustration on both sided and failure.

"At other times, reps will commit to an unreasonable amount of activity. When defining what's Measurable, always do the math and see if what they are saying makes sense. Salespeople committed to self-improvement tend to apply a realism filter to commitments they make, since they plan on following through.

Those who just want to get out of uncomfortable conversations tend to exaggerate in a way that might sound good in the moment, but won't lead to a reasonable output in their workday," Amir said.

"So when do you use the Action Plan? Do I present the Challenge, Outline the opportunity and then ask the salesperson to come up with an Action Plan? I'm confused about the order," Arlo said.

"Good question. You actually have some flexibility. Identifying the Challenge is your job as a coach; this is prior to the coaching conversation. After all, your goal is to create progress. And since you understand the gap between where they are now and where they need to be, Outlining the opportunity is your responsibility prior to the conversation as well," Amir explained.

"Okay, that makes sense," Arlo said. "Then what?"

"Then you have a decision to make. As you approach the conversation, you can decide—once you present the Challenge to your sales rep in conversation—whether or not you will discuss with them and co-create an Action Plan or task them with coming up with their own plan. It really depends upon the complexity of the Challenge and the experience of the sales rep.

"For instance, prior to attending the Leadership Conference, Alex identified that I could be doing a better job of growing people on my team and creating promotion opportunities. At present, they are not clear on the expectations and milestones necessary to be eligible to move up in the organization, and, if I'm being honest, I am typically so focused on the numbers that I don't spend an appropriate amount of time mentoring top performers on the team. We identified this as an opportunity, and I went to the conference with this in mind. Now, you're going to help me sift through my conference takeaways to create a MET Action Plan. I'll share it with Alex on Friday.

"When in doubt about a sales rep's ability to come up with a viable Action Plan, I always create it along with them."

"You mean you build it out for them?" Arlo said.

"No, definitely not. It's not *my* plan, it's theirs. If I build it for them, then I can't hold them accountable to it, and they'll have no buy in. Worse, I'll always be building their plans. They won't grow and I won't have time to do anything else!" Arlo realized why he always felt so overwhelmed by coaching conversations, and then frustrated by his reps' lack of follow-through.

"How do you create it with them?" he asked.

"We're salespeople! It's easy." Amir slid a laminated sheet across the table to Arlo. "I use the same *questioning techniques* that I ask my salespeople to use in the discovery process of a sales call. Even if I know exactly what needs to happen, I still need to ask questions in order to get the salesperson's buy in. Just like with a prospect, there is a big difference between me telling the rep that they need to do something and the rep identifying it themselves."

"Do you understand the additional benefit of using the very same techniques you ask your salespeople to use in their conversations?"

"I would think that it reinforces the behavior and demonstrates the technique."

"Very good." Amir nodded. "It also gives the salesperson the unique opportunity to understand what it feels like to be in the prospect's shoes. That helps to develop empathy as well as conviction that the method works."

"That's amazing," Arlo said, reading through the techniques on the list.

"Indeed it is." Amir smiled. "What you'll find, after consistently facilitating the conversation, is that reps become very competent at identifying their own Challenges and presenting the Action Plan to overcome them. That's when the framework really comes to life in a company."

Arlo put the pen down and rested his head in his hand. "I've got a lot of work to do," he sighed.

"Not until you help me with my Action Plan!" Amir playfully punched his shoulder.

They spent the next fifteen minutes pouring over Amir's notes and found three activities he could employ that would impact his

Challenge of not effectively mentoring his team. They worked together to define a MET Action Plan:

1. Learn the short-term and long-term professional goals of each sales rep.
2. Schedule lunch every other month with each sales rep to discuss their career goal attainment role and not just their performance numbers.
3. Identify opportunities like the Leadership Conference that would be relevant to each sales rep annually.

MEASURABLE
EMPOWERED
TIME - SENSITIVE

1. learn the short-term and long-term professional goals of each sales rep
2. schedule lunch every other month with each sales rep to discuss their career goal attainment role not just their performance numbers
3. identifying opportunities like the Leadership Conference relevant to each sales rep annually

As Arlo left for his office, he began to frantically send calendar requests to members of his team for later that day. He had a plan of his own.

Arlo Wrote The Third Secret: *Action Plan* in his journal.

Arlo had spent the whole of the day revisiting conversations with every rep on his team. He couldn't go on another minute with the knowledge that he was contributing to chaos. First he took the morning to evaluate each Challenge, dutifully lining them up along the MAStery framework.

SALESPERSON	CHALLENGES (BIGGEST IN BOLD)
SETH	· FAILS TO APPLY THE SKILLS HE SHOULD HAVE BEEN LEARNING IN TRAINING (SKILLSET)
DEREK	· LACKS TIME MANAGEMENT SKILLS (SKILLSET) · THINKS TALKING A LOT IN MEETINGS SHOWS OFF HIS KNOWLEDGE OF DEALS (MINDSET) · PREPS TOO MUCH FOR DEMOS, BUT DOESN'T FOCUS DEMO ON PAIN (ACTIVITY)
LINDSAY	· **THINKS AS LONG AS SHE SELLS, NOTHING ELSE MATTERS (MINDSET)** · HAS A BAD ATTITUDE INTERNALLY WITH TEAMMATES (MINDSET) · PRESSURES PROSPECTS TO BUY (MINDSET)
SAMANTHA	· **DOES NOT BELIEVE THAT PUTTING IN FULL DAYS IS NECESSARY (MINDSET)** · DOES NOT HIT PROSPECTING GOALS (ACTIVITY)

Then he began to Outline the path to success for each rep. The Outlines came easy to him, as he had now persuaded himself to create clarity around one specific Challenge and determine if it was related to Mindset, Activity, or Skillset.

When he was done, he pulled each of his salespeople into individual meetings. With prolific use of the whiteboard, he co-created Action Plans with each member of his team. It was a thing of beauty. It worked like magic!

As Amir had said, he felt the process getting easier and easier until he was truly in *the zone* by the end of the day. In most cases, the sales reps were able to co-create reasonable MET Actions, though the jury was out on Samantha.

The coaching conversation was definitely better than any other he'd had with her, but he wasn't convinced that she was truly committed to the Action Plan. She liked to quote the axiom, "Work smarter, not harder." Although from his vantage point, she really just clung to the "not harder" part. *We'll see how this pans out.*

12

THE FOURTH SECRET: C IS FOR CONSEQUENCES

*Most managers and salespeople alike want to be done with
the coaching conversation by the time an Action Plan is
agreed upon.*

Cora, like the other GigaTech managers, was right on time. Arlo
recognized her from mornings at the CupAJoe Cafe. He had
looked up her profile while on the Metro that morning and was
blown away. Ivy League education, including an MBA, she had
gone on from B-school to one of the big management consulting
firms, where she worked on government innovation projects in
emerging nations.

She had bounced out to tech, after leaving the management consulting firm, for a company based in Monterrey, Mexico where she
had led the North American account executive team until they
were acquired by GigaTech two years ago. Now she ran the inter-
national sales team.

She was cordial and definitely not at all like the managers he'd met so far. She reminded him more of the data scientists at VizuData. She was short. All she carried was a small laptop, and she navigated the maze of desks like someone moving through a crowd at a concert. A little haphazard, but making progress. As they rounded a corner to the conference room with 13 etched in the door, he caught a glimpse of Alex's dark office.

Suddenly he froze.

"Arlo, are you okay?" Cora asked. Arlo had stopped dead in his tracks just outside of the conference room, remembering only now that Alex had said not to roll anything out to his team until her return. What had he done? He had been so proud of himself for diving in. He could not afford a setback now. He was hanging by a thread.

"Yes, I'm fine." He picked up the pace and sat down across from Cora. "I should tell you that these secrets really make a ton of sense," he began, clearing his throat.

"Yes, I think so too," Cora said in a quiet voice as she focused intently on her computer. She didn't look up as Arlo sat there waiting patiently. She was obviously looking for something.

"After talking with Amir yesterday about Action Plans," he said, throat dry, "I went back to my office, identified the Challenges for each member of my team, Outlined the opportunities they have, and then I met with each one in the afternoon to create Action Plans."

"And then?" she said, still searching the laptop and not looking up.

"Then? Well then I guess I told them that I had faith in each of them and set them off to go to it!" He gave a small laugh.

Cora looked up from the laptop, unamused. "That's it?"

What is she talking about? He was feeling defensive. *Should I have taken them all to happy hour? Geez—yeah, that's it!* "Uh, yeah. That's it," he said.

Cora shook her head slowly from side to side and made a tsk-tsk sound as she seemed to have found what she was looking for. She spun the laptop to face him and leaned over the top. On the screen, he saw a simple spreadsheet with a person's name on each tab.

"What's this?" he asked.

"Read the labels on each row," she said.

"Challenge, Opportunity, Action, Conseq . . ."

"CONSEQUENCE, Arlo." She tapped the top of the screen with her pen like a piano teacher with a conductor's baton.

He gulped. It appeared he may have gotten ahead of himself. "Consequence," he said, biting his lip.

"The fourth secret is Consequence," Cora said, all business. "And it's an important one. What do you think it means?"

"The consequence for a failed Action Plan?" He was annoyed with himself, but felt like an insider using the language properly.

"Not exactly." Cora sounded a little annoyed. "Look, what you've done so far with your team is great, don't get me wrong. You're just lacking a few essential elements. One of which is clarity."

"Clarity?" he asked, cracking open his notebook and searching for a fresh page.

"Yes. Remember that the only failure as an outcome of an Action Plan is a failure to do the work" she said. "So the plan itself is not result-oriented, it is activity-based."

"Right." Arlo was running through the conversations from the day before in his mind. He was certain that all of the Action Plans were tied specifically to MET goals. "I was sure to use the MET framework when helping to facilitate Action Plans."

"Okay then," she exhaled, relieved. "What you did not do was specify the Consequence for not executing the plan. It's not surprising. Most managers and salespeople alike want to be done with the coaching conversation by the time an Action Plan is agreed upon."

She was right about that. He felt like he'd blown it and wanted to be done with this conversation.

"But that does a disservice to the effort both parties have expended in the conversation." Her tone was softening. "So it's essential that you make clear the Consequences for inaction. Those Consequences should be the consequence to the business, as well as the consequence for the individual in their role, and, if you're really good . . . the personal consequence."

"Personal consequence? What do you mean?" he asked.

"Here," Cora moved the laptop between them, "Not everyone likes spreadsheets, but they are kind of my thing," she said apologetically, as though she'd said it many times before. "Let's look at this sales rep." She pointed to the first person on the spreadsheet.

Arlo followed the row she'd highlighted. "Challenge: Afraid of using video in post-demo e-mails."

"We are trying to use video to reinforce pain points and key differentiators after demos to create velocity. I've tasked the team with using short video clips with strategic accounts," she said. "I identified it as a Mindset Challenge because I think the reluctance is based upon a fear of looking dumb."

"That makes sense to me. Outline: Ensure appropriate training. Review external conversion data. Practice before sending. Develop weekly activity frequency," he read aloud.

"Yup. That was my Outline for the conversation. The path to success that made sense to me," she said. "Go on."

"Action plan: 1) review software how-to by Friday. 2) Read two articles on video effectiveness in outbound and synthesize for the team by Monday. 3) Send five practice videos to Cora for different target personas by Tuesday. 4) Begin sending two videos per day, every day, by Wednesday. 5) Review conversion rates one week from Wednesday." He paused. It sounded like a very solid plan.

"Now. At this point, what is missing is clarity around what happens if the rep does not follow the Action Plan." She highlighted the next column.

Arlo continued, "Consequence: 1) Continued poor conversion on outbound to strategic accounts. 2) Likely failure to add strategic account revenue to pipeline. 3) Potential failure to meet quarterly revenue target. 4) Missing commission opportunity which is to be used for summer vacation."

Cora was quiet.

"Wow." Arlo sat back in his chair and folded his arms, thinking. Then he said, "So you are able to have a conversation with the sales rep about the impact to the business, to the department, and to the individual—if they fail to execute the Action Plan. That's powerful."

"It's clarity," she said. "It's my responsibility to articulate it. Sales is a tough profession; it's not enough to just task your team with doing things. They need to know why it's important to the business, why it is important to them professionally, and why it is important to them personally."

"So then, if they fail to execute on the Action Plan, the resulting conversation is easy," he said.

"Sure. Look down here," the pointer moved further down the row to another sales rep.

He read aloud, "Consequence: 1) Inability to generate enough qualified pipeline to cover quota. 2) Termination for failure to meet 90 percent of quota two quarters in a row." He paused. "So you just spell it out like that?"

"Of course. I don't want to have a surprise conversation with a rep at the end of the quarter regarding something that could have been discussed well in advance. That's not fair to either of us. When managers do that, the conversation is so uncomfortable that they stall or delay having it. You know what happens then?"

"Not exactly," he said.

"You end up with a bunch of poor performers on your team at great cost to the business, as well as to team and individual morale."

Arlo thought about Jackie. Her digs at her peers were affecting the team dynamic, but then he was equally to blame for letting poor performers like Maximillian stick around so long. Who wants to be working their butt off next to someone who is phoning it in?

"Keep in mind though, it's important to match the severity of the consequence to the impact of the Challenge. Not everything merits a conversation about whether or not someone will lose their job.

"Let's look at one more," she said.

"Consequence: 1) Increased demonstration of commitment to leadership. 2) Eligibility to interview for senior account executive role next quarter." Arlo raised his eyebrows. "How is that a consequence? It sounds like a potential promotion."

"That's exactly what it is! This rep is crushing it. I want him to demonstrate more leadership on the team, so we created an Action Plan which involves finding and presenting best practices for social selling each week in our team meeting for five minutes. If the Action Plan is executed, he'll be at the top of my list of people to interview for internal promotion next quarter."

"So the Consequence can actually be positive?" Arlo puzzled. He had never thought of coaching being anything but corrective.

"Of course!" She laughed for the first time. "If you have a strong team, the Consequence could always be positive. Continuous improvement, marginal gains." He could see the management consultant in her coming out. "Besides, who wants to be the menacing manager always finding fault? That's awful for everyone involved."

She went on, "Many times, the Challenge is continued growth or expanding skills or opening a new market or selling a new or expanded product. Something that would be challenging for almost anyone in the role, and that's not a bad thing! These Challenges are easily tackled with this method."

He leaned forward, hands on knees and fingers interlaced. "What the Consequence does is allow you and the rep to stay focused on the long-term vision, while working through the near-term execution."

Cora stopped. She stared at the ceiling, tapping a pen to her lip like her brain was buffering data. She spun the laptop around and began typing. "That's good. Really good. I want to remember that. I never thought of it that way before," she said.

That sounded like a little redemption to Arlo.

Arlo Wrote The Fourth Secret: *Consequence* in his notebook.

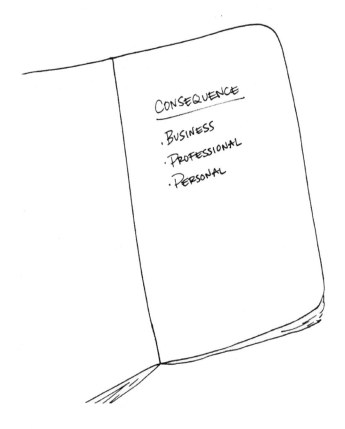

13

THE FIFTH SECRET: H IS FOR HOLD ACCOUNTABLE

When it comes to coaching, a lack of follow-through has devastating consequences. The implication is that the Action Plan is unimportant, or that the coach is disengaged and not invested in the success of the salesperson."

When Arlo stepped off the elevator on the forty-fifth floor on Friday morning, he was surprised to find Alex in the lobby talking to the receptionist.

"Hey, Arlo, I hear you've had quite a week." She smiled, looking at the clock. It was 6:55 a.m. "You got thirty minutes to run down your lessons learned with me after you meet with Hector this morning?"

Arlo found himself subconsciously straightening his posture. "It's been a great week. Thank you so much. Yes, of course I do," he said, fidgeting.

"Great. I'll be in conference room 23 getting ready for a meeting. Just poke your head in."

Hector appeared, strawberry-glazed donut in one hand, laptop in the other. He stuck out an elbow in lieu of a handshake. Arlo caught a glimpse of Paris, Rome, Istanbul, and Costa Rica stickers on the laptop and wondered if they were part of a wish list or a list of previous vacations.

"Arlo? Hey, nice to meet you." Hector took another bite of pink pastry.

They walked right around the corner to a conference room Arlo was surprised he hadn't noticed before. It was completely out of place in the mostly glass and bare wood design of GigaTech. Much bolder than the others, with walls painted in multi-colored graffiti, with what looked like a giant worm on the wall. On the door was a rainbow-painted "91." The room was disorienting, to say the least.

"This is my favorite conference room. Shakes things up a bit." He simulated the twist as he set his things down, "Forces you to get out of your comfort zone," Hector said.

"You can say that again," Arlo said, slowly taking it all in. He decided to keep his eyes trained on Hector to avoid distraction.

Hector was, by far, the oldest manager he'd met at GigaTech, probably fifteen years older than Alex, even though she was his boss.

He had greying temples and a glint in his eye that indicated, maybe, that he'd seen it all before.

His online profile revealed that he'd come up the ranks from inside sales manager years ago to sales operations, and now he headed up sales enablement for the company. He had published a lot of articles on sales process, metrics, and alignment of sales and marketing. In fact, he was pretty active on ConnectIn, with a ton of followers and a lot of opinions.

Using those old SDR research skills, Arlo had also found Hector's old personal blog on gluten-free, healthy eating. He smirked at the image of that pink donut going down and assumed Hector had moved on from that cause.

"So, I understand that you've been introduced to four of the Five Secrets of a Sales Coach so far. Challenge Identification, Outlining the Opportunity, Action Plan, Consequence, and now I'm bringin' up the rear, eh?" he said, popping the last bite into his mouth.

"It looks that way!" Arlo kept his focus steady on the spot between Hector's eyebrows.

"Any idea what the final secret might be?" he asked, peering over clear-framed reading glasses and raising one eyebrow.

"Well, I'm pretty certain it starts with an H," Arlo smiled.

Hector laughed with his whole body while his forearms remained planted on the table, presumably for balance. "That would be correct. In fact, the Fifth Secret is Hold Accountable."

Arlo aggressively flipped through his notebook. He'd taken a ton of notes during the past week and was surprised to have just a few pages left blank. He found one and began to write.

Donut gone now, Hector struck a serious tone. "You know as well as anyone that the role of management involves executive meetings, cross-departmental meetings, team meetings, reports, hiring committees, impromptu requests, selling conversations, training." He paused for a breath. "And little time for things like following up on coaching conversations. So those things fall to the wayside."

Arlo knew all too well what Hector was referring to. He frequently had to push meetings because of a competing priority. That was just the nature of the role, he thought.

Hector leaned forward. "Well, Arlo, when it comes to coaching, a lack of follow-through has devastating consequences. The implication is that the Action Plan is unimportant, or that the coach is disengaged and not invested in the success of the salesperson."

"I once heard someone say 'inspect what you expect,'" Arlo offered.

"I've heard that too. But do you want to be the team inspector? Micromanaging details for other adults?" he said, as the eyebrow went up again.

Arlo shook his head. Put that way, it sounded like something he neither had time for nor interest in.

"Of course not. We want to develop our people into a level of accountability which requires direction not inspection." Hector leaned back, surveying Arlo.

"So, how do I do that?" Arlo said.

"Mutual accountability."

Arlo wrote it down. "Mutual accountability," he said, hoping to prompt a further explanation.

"That's correct. So simple that all you have to do is ask." Hector folded his arms in conclusion. But Arlo had no idea what this meant. So Hector continued.

"The best managers create clear accountability steps without creating homework for themselves. A rep's failure to perform should not create homework for you. A lot of managers profess to being 'there for their reps' or 'servant leaders' and end up resenting the fact that they're spending Saturday night covering while the rep is off partying at a music festival, boom-chh, boom-chh, boom-chh." He yelled and waved his arms like an inflatable-arm-flailing tube man trying to attract passers-by into a used car lot. It looked crazy!

"Okay, so. All I have to do is ask who, what exactly?" He squinted, trying to keep a straight face, hoping it made him look like he was endeavoring really hard to understand.

"Exactly!" Hector laughed again, folded arms resting on top of his heaving belly, dislodging a few pink crumbs. "Ah ha! Yes! That is the question!"

Wow this one is a little bit whacky.

"All you have to do is ask your sales rep, 'How can you keep me abreast of your progress so we can ensure you are on the right track?' and 'How can I support you to ensure your success?'" He spread his arms wide open now, as if he'd just finished a show tune with jazz hands.

"That's it?" Arlo said.

"What more is there?" asked Hector.

This was like Charlie and the Chocolate Factory or something. Arlo wasn't sure if that was a riddle, a rhetorical question, or a plea. So he sat quietly, fiddling with his pen, staring into his notebook, and trying to make sense of what Hector had just said.

Hector leaned back in his chair, hands on the table for balance, and stared at Arlo. He was clearly waiting for Arlo to realize the depth of what had just been said.

There they sat.

"Okay then." Arlo wasn't sure which was crazier—Hector or conference room 91, but it felt like the meeting was over.

Hector stood. "It is simple, but you *must* remember this Fifth Secret. A coaching relationship is based upon your consistent ability to hold someone accountable to specific Actions, and their consistent ability to trust that they have your commitment and support." He came around the table with a deadly serious face and placed a hand on Arlo's shoulder. "This is precisely where the coaching relationship thrives or dies."

With that, he was out the door. Only a lone, crumb of pink frosting remained where he sat.

Arlo still had forty-five minutes before he was supposed to meet Alex. He wrote down the two things he'd learned from Hector. The man was either crazy or a genius. The jury was still out.

Arlo wrote The Fifth Secret: *Hold Accountable* in his journal.

14

ARLO GETS C.O.A.C.H.ED

Everything should be made as simple as possible, but no simpler.

—*Albert Einstein*

Arlo leaned forward in his chair, studying his notebook, waiting for eight o'clock to roll around so he could meet Alex. After two complete cycles of reviewing his notes, he felt ten years wiser. In the context of his notes, he was now confident that Hector was actually a genius. He remembered an Albert Einstein quote from high school, "Everything should be made as simple as possible, but no simpler."

He had even begun to appreciate conference room 91, though clearly there should only be one conference room like this in the whole town. He was getting excited about sharing his lessons learned with Alex. He sensed it was time to reap the rewards with his own team.

The clock struck 8 a.m., and Arlo made his way to the grandest conference room of them all. Conference room 23. Alex sat in the middle of a long, glass conference table. Multiple screens adorned one wall and the rest were floor-to-ceiling windows, which gave the impression of being suspended in midair. A bird flew by below them. It was incredible.

"Grab a seat," Alex said, placing her pen on her legal pad and turning to face him. She had clearly been prepping for a meeting. "So, how did it go, Arlo?"

He remembered Amir's story of failing to answer this very question so he was prepared. "I made a page of bullets for you as promised." He shared the following pages from his notebook:

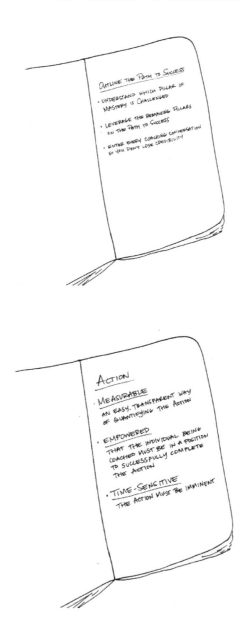

Outline the Path to Success

· Understand which Pillar of Mastery is Challenged

· Leverage the Remaining Pillars on the Path to Success

· Enter every Coaching Conversation so you don't lose credibility

Action

· Measurable
An easy, transparent way of quantifying the Action

· Empowered
That the individual being coached must be in a position to successfully complete the Action

· Time-Sensitive
The Action must be imminent

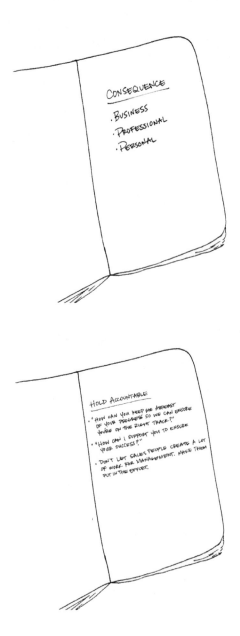

"Very impressive, Arlo. It looks like you've had a productive week!" she said.

"Your team has been really great. It was very generous of them to share their time," he said.

"It is actually part of our responsibility. When this framework was handed down to me, the only commitment I made was that I would actively seek out others who could benefit from it and share it with them too. I have asked the same of my team. And one day, I'll ask the same of you."

Arlo felt honored. He was committed to earning his stripes.

"I talked to a lot of managers before meeting you. Your team seems to be wired completely differently'," he said.

"In what way?" she asked.

"Most of the sales leaders I have met before could pretty easily fall into three tendencies. Granted not exclusively, but predominantly."

"Go on," Alex said, intrigued.

"Pilots—the type of managers who heavily leverage metrics and data; Heroes—the type who are great salespeople and love to do deals; and Cheerleaders—the ones who are great motivators. My frustration was that these personality types did not necessarily correlate to great coaching. They were just styles," he said

"Exactly right. By your definition, Charles is a hero, Olivia a cheerleader, and Cora is definitely a pilot."

"What about Amir and Hector?" he asked.

"Amir is new to management so he may not have developed a personality yet. And Hector? Well, he's been around for a long time and he's just crazy!" She laughed. "But in spite of their tenure or their management personality, they are all excellent coaches and rigorous practitioners of the framework. That's the beauty. When you employ a framework, it magnifies the strengths and supports the weaknesses of every coach."

"Which leads us to you, Arlo. Last week, when you stole my cortado, you were in a world of hurt before your management team meeting. What's changed?" she said.

"I've got some clear revenue targets for this quarter," he said.

"Clear revenue targets?"

"Yes, 20 percent over last quarter's goal, which my team missed. And over the next three quarters, we need to increase our average deal size by about 40 percent."

"It doesn't sound like the C.O.A.C.H. framework is something you could focus on in a quarter to move the needle on the number then," she said.

"No, it absolutely is!" he said. "I already, kind of prematurely, rolled it out with my team. I rolled out C, O, A—not thinking about the fact that the final C and H would probably be important," he admitted.

She was all business. "Okay, so you half-ass rolled out C.O.A.C.H. Even though I warned against doing so."

Arlo squirmed.

She smirked, half annoyed, but also happy to see how committed Arlo was to self-improvement and actually adopting what he was learning. "How are you going to fully rollout the framework? Quickly?"

"My plan is to have meetings with each individual on Monday, revisit the Action Plan, and introduce the Consequence and how we'll old one another accountable," he said.

"How will you ensure that you keep track of the Action Plans, Consequences, and your ability to Hold folks Accountable?"

"I really like Cora's spreadsheet. She actually sent me the template. I'm assuming that you know about this one?" he said.

"Yes, I'm familiar." She was not-so-subtly indicating that she was the mastermind behind the elegant and efficient way of keeping coaching momentum from week to week. "Very good! Once you've got it all in the spreadsheet, how will you ensure that you keep your commitments if it includes follow-up meetings or information reviews?"

"I thought of that. I've cleared three hours in my calendar each week—blocked off specifically for that purpose. I'll be sure that those activities take place in those time frames."

"That's a great idea. What happens if you get busy or fail to create momentum from week to week?"

"I'll be back where I am at today, which is unacceptable. I can't let that happen," Arlo said with increasing confidence.

Alex pressed further. "What does that mean? 'Back where I am today . . .'"

Arlo looked directly at her. "I'll actually lose my job. I'll be fired, according to my boss." It hurt to say it out loud. At the same time, that helpless feeling was gone. For the first time, Arlo felt in control of his own destiny. He had a plan and he knew how to execute the plan.

Alex nodded, signaling approval. She leaned across her desk. Very slowly, she asked, "How can you keep me abreast of your progress so that I can ensure you are on the right track?" Her eyebrows were raised.

"I will shoot you an e-mail each week, giving you a high-level update on the success of the team." He could now clearly see what she was doing. She was coaching him. That was pretty cool.

"And you can support my success by just giving me feedback on my progress," he concluded.

She smiled. "Very good, then. That's what we'll do."

And that's what they did.

15

ARLO BECOMES A C.O.A.C.H.

*I think the most important thing about coaching is that you
have to have a sense of confidence about what you're doing.*

—*Phil Jackson*

The next eleven weeks passed with Arlo sending weekly high-
level updates to Alex as he had promised. She always responded
promptly with an acknowledgement of specific progress he had
noted in his update. She'd provide some guidance from her own
experience regarding his Action Plan for the week. Then she'd ask
one simple question: "How can I support you?"

They met monthly for fifteen minutes at CupAJoe's—he had developed a taste for cortados, much to Alex's amusement. He found
the fifteen minutes to be more than enough to bounce around
his ideas regarding the team Challenges he was focusing on as he

developed his Outlines. Alex was generous with her time, and he took pride in not needing too much of it.

The final week of the quarter, Arlo once again made his way to the forty-fifth floor for a final debrief with Alex. He was smiling to himself as the elevator doors opened.

"Hey, Arlo," Alex said, leading him back past the elevators to a little room he'd never noticed, off to the side of the elevator bank. The door had an old-school, grey sliding name plate on it that just said "Jackson."

The room was barely large enough for two people. In fact, it looked as though it had been completely missed by the GigaTech interior design team. No windows. Nothing fancy. Just a small wooden table and two old chairs. Arlo thought it was pretty austere for such a proud occasion.

They sat, and Arlo began, "I know I keep telling you this, but I just can't thank you enough. I feel as though my entire world has opened up and I can finally have the impact I've always imagined."

Arlo had been meticulous in his adherence to the C.O.A.C.H. framework. In fact, he'd initially over-prepared for every conversation, accustomed to the over-engineered and ruthlessly complex "sales methodologies" and "performance measurement" tools companies he'd worked for had rolled out every year with their charts, decks, diagrams, and metrics that were quickly abandoned by anyone who actually had a job to do.

Instead, he felt confident coaching right out of the gate. It was so similar to the skills he learned in sales—identifying pain, reverse-engineering the close, agreeing upon the next steps, being a partner instead of an adversary . . . it fit like a glove.

"What do you mean, exactly?" Alex asked, seeming to know the answer already.

"I feel confident," he said. That was it. And he deserved it. He had more than anyone could have imagined in a single quarter. He gave Alex the specifics.

Arlo had discovered that Seth had a skill challenge. So he quickly provided training on how to uncover pain during discovery. It was like a light suddenly went on. Seth found relief in not having to educate and do the kind of convincing he had done as a community organizer. He quickly learned how to ask questions, listen, and diagnose.

Seth's next challenge was learning how to run an effective demo without focusing on features and benefits. Arlo identified that this was a mindset challenge and Seth committed to eliminating his demo script and only presenting to the pain he uncovered. It took some practice, and there were some comedic moments of silence, with Seth grimacing to avoid feature-jumping. But his conversion rate skyrocketed.

Samantha began offering yoga twice a week to the team during lunch—in order to build a client following of co-workers and their friends. It was Samantha's idea, which she had been scared to ask about until Arlo addressed her activity challenge regarding being otherwise committed. He'd simply asked if there was a way she could connect her sales role to her yoga aspirations.

Arlo then suggested that her ability to understand people and uncover the challenges they are facing might be impactful as a business owner. Samantha's mindset had been that yoga had nothing to do with sales. She now felt that the sales conversations she had all day with small business owners actually helped her to understand working professionals. She was making way more money than she had ever thought possible too. So she decided to partner with an existing studio, keep her job, and create after-hours yoga programming for professionals.

Derek, it turns out, had an activity challenge. His shiny object obsession left him failing to execute. So Arlo coached him on controlling the quantity and quality of his activities and monitoring the results that these produced. As a result, he was able to develop leading indicators (such as pipeline coverage ratio) that let him know when he was at risk of not hitting his number; but knew in advance, so he had time to make changes.

Arlo and Derek also collaborated on creating specific projects with finite activities and timelines that would allow Derek his opportunity to explore new ideas without jeopardizing his core goals.

Arlo thought that Jackie was going to be his biggest challenge. Her performance was formidable, and she wasn't much of a team player. He found that two things turned her around—not completely, but enough to be tolerable.

First, Arlo went to work on her mindset that the team was beneath her. He asked her how she grew junior teammates when she was captain of her volleyball team. Jackie committed to contributing constructive and specific feedback instead of antagonizing, and agreed to let Arlo use her calls in training to help her build back the respect of the team.

The monumental change with Jackie came when the team itself began to rise. As her colleagues demonstrated more focus, accountability, and results—Jackie seemed to feel much more of a sense of camaraderie. The team had even begun to go to her for advice. The day Arlo looked over his monitor and saw Seth and Jackie in a conference room over a laptop, laughing hysterically, he was certain that the earth had shifted on its axis.

Perhaps the biggest surprise was Lindsay. Before meeting Alex, Arlo hadn't thought that coaching Lindsay was necessary. She was who she was. She got the job done. Just average. But consistent.

Boy, was he wrong! When he learned from Cora that coaching was not all about punitive consequences, but could be about opportunities, he had an idea for Lindsay. He had a conversation with her about what her goals were. It turned out that she had really wanted his job. When she didn't get it, she had been deflated. She wasn't aware that her performance had leveled out; she just felt she was doing what she'd always done.

So they made an Action Plan. Arlo shared with her that if the VizuData was able to prove out the ability to sell bigger SMB deals, they would be adding to the team, which meant adding a manager on the east coast. She switched into another gear.

Her sales were not only double her quota for the quarter, she developed a demo training program and started working with marketing on webinars for a new vertical. She was not going to miss this opportunity for promotion. Lindsay and Arlo had set aside a few hours per month for him to work with her on the skills she needed to be ready for the role when it was made available.

But Arlo saved the biggest news for last.

"I'm so happy for you, Arlo!" This was the most excitement he'd seen from Alex. She beamed with pride.

He raised an eyebrow and smiled a cocky grin. "There's more . . ."

She punched his shoulder. "Oh I know, I know . . . You got to your 40 percent deal size increase. Your CEO is elated. You're awesome . . . whatever, whatever . . ." She rolled her eyes.

He brushed imaginary dust from each shoulder. "Well yes, Alex, that's all true," he mocked, laughing, "but it's not the best part."

"Well, tell me!" she said eagerly.

"Remember when you said, 'When the student is ready, the teacher will appear?'"

She bit her lip. She knew what he was going to say.

"I'm teaching the C.O.A.C.H. framework to Lindsay now."

"Well I'll be damned, Rolo," she said sitting back in her chair in full admiration of the C.O.A.C.H. she had created. "That's what it's all about."

She sat for a few beats, just nodding appreciatively as Arlo beamed with pride.

"Okay. Back to work!" She broke the silence, rose, and shook Arlo's hand. As they turned to leave, he noticed a plaque in the shadows behind the door. It read:

> *"I think the most important thing about coaching is that you have to have a sense of confidence about what you're doing."*

> —Phil Jackson

Learn more about becoming a ClozeLoop certified sales coach at CoachFramework.com/certification.

Made in the USA
Las Vegas, NV
15 February 2022